GW00482601

Cooking with Love

Compiled by Lisa Gordon, Maria Lockhart, Nicola Williams.
Published by Cooking with Love.

Foreward

AFTER BEING INVOLVED in a number of fundraising events over the years, we wanted to do something to support two very special charities but at the same time break with the tradition of organising events which depend on a relatively small number of people pledging large amounts of money (normally with the help of a talented auctioneer and plenty of wine on the table!) We had the bright idea of combining our desire to do something worthwhile with our passion for food and "Cooking with Love" was born!

The idea of a charity cookbook is not new but we hope we have come up with something special. This book is about family, friendship and food....all the things that that make life worth living. It is a collection of recipes from enthusiastic cooks, ranging from everyday domestic god/goddesses to professional chefs. All the recipes are special. Some have been passed down from one generation to the next; others have become a firm favourite or a signature dish; but all evoke happy memories of meals shared with family and friends.

"Cooking with Love" has been produced to raise funds for two charities that do so much to help people when they need it most - Maggie's Cancer Caring Centres (Reg Charity No. SC024414) and

The Rainbow Trust Childrens' Charity (Reg Charity No. 1070532) which cares for terminally ill children and their families (more information on the charities can be found later in this book). On their behalf we would like to express our grateful thanks to all our sponsors and contributors and to those of you who have bought this book, for your support in enabling us to raise as much as possible for our chosen charities.

A project on this scale is not possible without the help of many people. At its formative stage the committee included Eva Davies and Nicky Blystad and they were instrumental in getting the project off the ground and we are grateful to them both for their continuing support.

When we launched ourselves into this project 18 months ago, we didn't realise that we had so much to learn about publishing a book. So many people generously devoted their time and services to help us deliver a book of this quality. We have gone up a very steep learning curve under the watchful eye of George Beverley, our designer and Mark Hogan of Heidelberg. Thank you both for leading us out of the publishing wilderness!

We are thrilled with the photographs of the dishes which are the genuine article, cooked by ourselves and photographed in Nicola's kitchen by Suzanne Newell.

The one area we were pretty confident about was the cooking and we all thought testing the recipes would be the fun bit, but whittling down 300 recipes to a final shortlist was more challenging that we might have imagined! Our thanks go to our dedicated team of testers who took their responsibilities very seriously. As a result of their efforts, we are pleased to tell you that all the recipes included in the book have been fully measured, tested, timed and work beautifully!

We hope you enjoy the recipes and the stories behind them. Thank you for supporting Maggie's and The Rainbow Trust and happy cooking!

Lisa Gordon, Nicola Williams, Maria Lockhart.

"Cooking is like love. It should be entered into with abandon or not at all."

~Harriet van Horne

"'the jetty' and I are delighted to support this fantastic Cook Book which celebrates the love of food, in aid of two great causes which are close to many peoples hearts.

Too often we underestimate the power of a touch, a smile, a kind word, a listening ear, an honest compliment, or the smallest act of caring, all of which have the potential to turn a life around.

'the jetty' is open to all and has a huge varied clientele we greet with open arms."

Alex Aitken - Restaurateur

About the charities

Rainbow Trust Children's Charity provides emotional and practical support to families who have a child with a life threatening or terminal illness. Rainbow Trust's Family Support Workers join the family in their own home and are there to provide practical support. We are contactable 24 hours a day for families in crisis from diagnosis, through treatment and even after bereavement. Rainbow relies almost entirely on voluntary donations and through the generosity of our supporters we are able to help around 1,000 families a year.

This year Rainbow Trust celebrates its 25th anniversary. Founded in 1986, we have now supported thousands of families who have a child with a life threatening or terminal illness. With the help of the families who share their inspirational stories about the difference Rainbow has made to their lives, we have been able to raise our profile and tell more people about the work that we do.

Maggie's Oxford Campaign

Maggie's is a cancer organisation with a difference. They provide a highly personalised cancer care programme in a very special environment: supportive, practical, welcoming and a complete contrast to the hospital next door.

A Maggie's Centre is a welcoming, friendly and non-institutional place, adjacent to a cancer treatment hospital, which provides support for people with any kind of cancer, their families, friends and carers. Maggie's supports people from the moment they ask for help, free of charge, and unconditionally for as long as help is needed.

Individual visitors can access information on cancer and its treatment, emotional support, confidential counselling and advice. They can also join regular timetabled group activities, such as relaxation and visualisation courses, nutrition workshops, and support groups. The staff at Maggie's are all experienced Clinical Nurse Specialists or Clinical Psychologists with expertise in individual and group counselling

Anyone can drop into a Maggie's Centre without a formal referral from medical staff and everything at Maggie's is provided free of charge.

Acknowledgements

With grateful thanks to the following for their support in producing this book

PRC

The Oratory School

Paul Burrows of The Highwayman, Checkendon

Mark Hogan, Heidelberg

George Beverley & Laura Walker, Designers

Antony Worrall Thompson

Liz Huysinga

Jane Newton

Suzanne Marshall, Yattendon Group

Terry Lipscombe, Vision Paper and Board Ltd

All those who submitted recipes

Our advertisers

Our testers:

Emma Armstrong

Gill Austin

Juliet Baxter

Nicky Blystad

Karen Birkholm

Juliet Coleman

Eva Davies

Maria Fernandez de Pinedo

Elizabeth Green

Kate Hamilton-Bowker

Belinda Hill

Sarah Ingram

Robyn Jones

Jane Kibble

Steve Knott

Helen McAllister

Anna Mason

Billie Richards

Juliet Smeeton

...and our own families who were immensely patient and supportive throughout this 18 month project.

The recipes in this book have been reproduced by kind permission of their contributers. Suzanne Newell was our photographer and the photographs are reproduced with her kind permission. Copyright in the photographs is owned by Suzanne Newell. The members of the Cooking With Love Committee created the design and layout of the book and reserve their rights in the work. First published 2011.

Published by Cooking with Love. Photography by Suzanne Newell.

Index

Soups and Starters

Fish

Chicken

Game

Meat

Index

Vegetarian

Hot Puddings

Cold Puddings

Cakes and Cookies

Bits and Bobs

Starter and Soups

Pancetta and Chestnut Soup

This is one of the easiest soups to make and is enthused over every time! A delicious starter, or warming lunch-time meal. A winner every time.

 Serves 4  Preparation time 10 mins 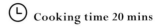 Cooking time 20 mins

Ingredients:

2 tbsp olive oil

2 tbsp butter

100g pancetta, chopped

2 large onions, finely chopped

435g tin chestnut purée

300mls chicken stock

300mls double cream

salt and pepper

Method

Heat the oil and butter in a large pan on a gentle heat, add the pancetta pieces and fry until the fat begins to run. Remove the pancetta and set aside.

Add the onion to the fat and cook until very soft but not coloured. When the onions are soft add the remaining ingredients and bring the soup just up to boiling point.

Add the pancetta and simmer for a few minutes.
Taste for seasoning.

The soup can be liquidised if you prefer it smooth, and if you prefer a soup that is slightly less rich, you can reduce the amount of cream and increase the stock.

Jane Kibble

Butternut Squash , Lime and Ginger Soup

I first had this soup after a big October surf in Cornwall. It was made by a friend and enjoyed with a table full of cheeses and crusty bread. Having battled with the elements we were a well deserving "crew". It was quite simply the best soup I had ever tasted, and I have been making it ever since.

 Serves 6 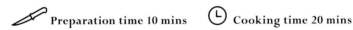 Preparation time 10 mins   Cooking time 20 mins

Ingredients:

1 tbsp olive oil

2 onions, chopped

5cm fresh ginger, chopped

pinch of dried chilli

1 clove of garlic

1 butternut squash, peeled
   and chopped

juice and zest of 1 or 2 limes

1 litre vegetable stock

Method

Heat the oil in a large pan and sauté the onions for a few minutes until they are translucent. Add the squash, ginger, chilli and garlic and cook for a further few minutes making sure they don't stick by stirring from time to time!

Add the lime zest and enough stock to just cover. Simmer until the squash is soft then add the lime juice. When the vegetables are cooked add more stock just to make the soup the way you like it! You can always add milk, cream, or stock to thin it.

Whisk and add pepper and a touch of coriander to garnish.

Nicky Clayton

Carrot and Coriander Soup with Crème Fraîche

This is essentially a lovely warming winter soup which is so tasty whilst at the same time feels very fresh. It makes an interesting change from the rather over familiar recipes for carrot soup. I also like the fact that you can control the thickness of the soup according to the temperature outside.

 Serves 6    **Preparation time 10 mins**   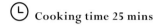 **Cooking time 25 mins**

Ingredients:

3 tbsp olive oil

2 onions, skinned and chopped

6 medium carrots, peeled
    and chopped

900mls chicken or vegetable stock

sea salt

freshly ground black pepper

a grating of nutmeg

juice of ½ lemon

2 good handfuls of coriander

150mls full-fat Crème Fraîche

Method

Heat the olive oil in a saucepan and add the onions. Sauté until they are soft and start to colour. Add the chopped carrots and cook for about 5 minutes, stirring occasionally, so that the carrots begin to caramelise on the surface.

Add the stock, season with salt, pepper and nutmeg. Bring the liquid to simmering point and cook gently for about 20 minutes or until the biggest piece of carrot is tender.

Allow it to cool, then liquidize with the lemon juice, coriander and crème fraîche. You can garnish with a teaspoon of crème fraîche.

Juliet Baxter

Carrot and Coriander Soup with Crème Fraîche

Watercress and Potato Soup

I adapted this recipe years ago when my children, Amy and Tom, were knee-high to grasshoppers, in an attempt to get them to eat something packed with iron that actually tasted good too.

 Serves 2-4  **Preparation time 15 mins** 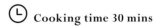 **Cooking time 30 mins**

Ingredients:

4 bunches of watercress

2 large potatoes

1 small onion, chopped

425mls vegetable stock

150mls milk

knob of butter

salt and pepper to taste

Method

Chop the onions, potatoes and watercress. Heat a knob of butter in a large pan and sauté the onion until softened, but not brown. Add the watercress, potato, stock and milk and simmer for 15 minutes. Allow to cool.

Liquidize and return to the pan. Heat thoroughly but do not allow to boil.

Serve with a garnish sprig of watercress and fresh bread.

For extra flavour try adding bacon or leeks.

John Barnard

Chorizo and Butternut Soup

My mother gave me this recipe when I was complaining about having to cook another casserole for a shoot lunch. It is a meal in itself and is a warming and filling lunch on a cold day.

 Serves 6  **Preparation time 30 mins** **Cooking time 30 mins**

Ingredients:

2 tbsp olive oil

1 onion chopped

2 cloves of garlic finely chopped

225g chorizo diced

1 large red chilli chopped

2 x cans 400g tomatoes

1 tbsp dark brown sugar

1 red pepper de-seeded and chopped

1 butternut squash de-seeded and diced

410g can of cannellini beans drained and washed

parsley

Method

Heat the oil in a saucepan and cook the onion and garlic until soft. Add the chorizo and red chilli and cook until the chorizo releases its juices. Add the tomatoes, pepper, sugar and 150mls cold water. Cover and simmer for 10 minutes.

Stir in the butternut squash, cover and simmer for 45 minutes, stirring occasionally, until the squash is tender.

Add the cannellini beans and simmer for 5 minutes.

Stir in the parsley just before serving.

Freezes well.

Nick and Sarah Brown

16

Real Tomato Soup

Nothing beats "real" tomato soup at any time of the year, and it is a great way to use your home grown produce when they take off in the garden and just keep on coming.

 Serves 6

Ingredients:

1kg fresh tomatoes

1 potato, peeled and cut into small chunks

2 tbsp olive oil

2 cloves of garlic

2 tsp sugar

salt and pepper

Garnish

fromage frais (lower on calories than cream)

a little chopped parsley or basil

Method

Pre-heat oven to 190C.

Add half the oil to the roasting tin and spread over the base of the tin. Cut all the tomatoes in half and spread out in the roasting tin. Add the garlic cloves and pour the rest of the oil over the tomatoes. Sprinkle with salt and pepper. Put in the oven for 30 minutes.

While the tomatoes are roasting, boil the potato in 300mls of water. When it is cooked, use a fork to take out the potato and keep the water to one side.

Take the tomatoes out of the oven and take off their skins which are now really easy to remove with a fork. Put everything into the food processor – tomatoes, garlic, sugar and potato plus water and blend it all until it is smooth.

The soup is now ready and just needs to be heated up in a saucepan. A drop of fromage frais and a sprinkling of chopped parsley or basil adds to the flavour and makes it more attractive to serve to guests.

Gordon Brown MP and Sarah Brown

Artichoke and Green Olive Tapenade

A few years ago I purchased a delicious tapenade at a French store specialising in olives. When they stopped making it, I decided to try for myself and here is the result, very easy to make - and a sure winner. Serve on tiny pieces of toast or crackers with champagne, dry white wine or sherry.

 Serves 10-15    Preparation time 10 mins

Ingredients:

1 tin artichoke hearts, finely chopped

1 tin green pitted olives, finely chopped

juice of ½ lemon

plenty of good virgin olive oil

dash of cayenne pepper

fresh rosemary (optional)

Method

Put the chopped artichoke hearts and olives in a food processor. Pour in the lemon juice and enough olive oil to get efficient chopping. Add the rosemary if you like the taste. Process and continue adding olive oil until you get the right consistency. Add cayenne pepper to taste towards the end. You can increase the olive taste of the tapenade by using more green olives.

The tapenade can be made days before you need it, keep it in a closed jar in the fridge.

Mimi Rode Wiik

Egg, Chives and Cream Cheese with Arctic Caviar

This starter presents really beautifully on a plain white dish and is delicious. Dinner guests help themselves to a piece of this stunning "cake". You should be able to find Arctic caviar in decent sized supermarkets. It is original and different.

 Serves 6-8    Preparation time 20 mins   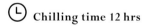 Chilling time 12 hrs

Ingredients:

7 hard boiled eggs

4 tbsp mayonnaise

1 pack parsley chopped

2 packs chives chopped

300g philadelphia cheese with chives

Arctic caviar - preferably the orange version

Method

Take the Philadelphia cheese out of the fridge and leave at room temperature to soften. You can spread it out a bit in a bowl to speed up the process.

Finely chop the hard boiled eggs, add the mayonnaise and the chopped parsley. Spread this to cover the inner base of a deepish dinner plate.

Finely chop the chives and cover the layer of egg. Spread the soft Philadelphia over the chives using a spatula. Cover and leave in the fridge overnight. Just before serving, spread the Arctic caviar over the top.

This is delicious and looks great passed round with a cake knife so that each guest can cut themselves a slice. Serve with Melba toast. You can also serve with a bowl of crème fraîche to accompany the dish.

Anicken Lundgaard

Harissa Houmous with Fennel Pitta Crisps

This has been my most popular canapé amongst all our friends. The spicy taste is really complimented by the pitta toasts. Not only does it taste great but is also low in fat and nutritious. The intensity of the colours gives the presentation a real wow factor.

 Serves 10    **Preparation time 20 mins**   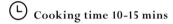 **Cooking time 10-15 mins**

Ingredients:

Houmous

2 x 400g cans chickpeas,
    rinsed and drained

5 tbsp olive oil

1 garlic clove, crushed

lemon juice, to taste

2 tbsp Belazu Rose
    Harissa paste

1 tbsp tomato purée

Fennel pitta crisps

6 pitta breads

3-5 tbsp olive oil

1 tbsp fennel seeds

pinch of sea salt

Method

Pre-heat the oven to 190C.

To make the houmous, put ¾ of the chickpeas in a food processor with 3 tablespoons of olive oil, garlic and half a cupful of water. Blitz until smooth, adding a little more water if necessary to make a thick cream consistency. Add the rest of the chickpeas, then whiz again for a few seconds until it has a knobbly texture. Season with salt and add a good squeeze of lemon juice. Transfer to a serving dish.

In a clean bowl mix together the harissa paste and tomato purée with the rest of the olive oil and drizzle over the houmous.

To make the pitta crisps, split each pitta bread horizontally into 2 circles and cut each into 6 triangles. Place the triangles in a resealable plastic bag, add the olive oil, salt and fennel seeds and shake until the triangles are lightly coated.

Lay them in a single layer on 2 or 3 baking sheets. Bake for 10-15 minutes until golden and leave to cool.

Karen Birkholm

Crab Dip

For my friends who like it hot! I randomly threw this together one day and although it is different every time I make it, it never fails. Add as much or as little spice as your friends can take.

 Serves 6-8   Preparation time 10 mins

Ingredients:

1 tin white crab meat or
    equivalent fresh

1 tsp Thai red curry paste

1 tsp Mirin (rice wine)

1 tbsp spring onions, chopped

1 tbsp fresh coriander, chopped

juice of ½ lime

120mls coconut milk

Method

Mix all ingredients together in a large bowl.

Chill before serving.

Roz Kempner

Fishy Pots

We love having people over for easy suppers and this is one starter I always revert back to. We are all so busy these days so it has to be easy. The ingredients are easy to get hold of, can come out of the freezer, it is easy to cook, and the dish served hot on a winter's day seems perfect.

 Serves 6-8   Preparation time 20 mins

Ingredients:

1 large or 2 small smoked
    haddock fillets

½ bottle of dry white wine

350mls good quality fish stock

1 packet of raw tiger prawns

5 scallops

50g butter

50g flour

parsley

Method

Mix the wine and the stock in a saucepan. Add the fish, making sure the liquid covers it, and bring to the boil. Cover and simmer for 3 minutes until the meat flakes off the skin. Remove, discard the skin and cover.

Add the tiger prawns to the liquid and boil until pink and cooked. Remove and put with the fish.

Add the scallops and cook for one minute (or until cooked), remove and put with the fish and prawns and cover.

In a separate pan melt the butter and add flour and cook for about a minute. Add the fish liquid to make a sauce, boil for a few minutes. Add the cooked fish, scallops, prawns, and chopped parsley, lots of freshly ground black pepper and serve in heated ramekin dishes.

Sarah Cameron

Chicken Liver Pâté Brûlée

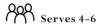 **Serves 4-6**

Ingredients:

*450g chicken or duck livers,
    trimmed and cleaned*

175g unsalted butter, softened

2 shallots, finely chopped

1 tsp soft thyme leaves

2 cloves garlic, finely chopped

2 tbsp brandy

2 tbsp anchovy essence

½ tsp ground black pepper

*50g clarified butter, melted
    (optional)*

4-6 tsp caster sugar

Method

Heat 1 tablespoon of butter in a frying pan until foaming. Add half the livers and fry quickly on all sides until golden, but still pink in the middle, about 4-5 minutes. Repeat with second batch of livers. Place livers and any juices in a food processor.

In the same pan heat another tablespoon of butter and add the shallots, thyme and garlic and cook over a moderate heat until the shallots are soft but have not coloured. Add brandy, anchovy essence and pepper and scrape the bottom of the pan to release any coagulated juices. Place everything in the food processor including the remaining butter. Blend until smooth.

If you want a very smooth paté pass the mixture through a fine sieve and put in a bowl. Then fill small espresso cups with the mixture. Cover with cling film, cool and then refrigerate.

Once refrigerated, dust the tops of the cups with caster sugar and carefully blast with blow torch, as you would for crème brulée, so the surface is nicely caramelised, or top with clarified butter and chill.

Serve with Crostini.

Antony Worrall Thompson - Chef

"I randomly threw this together
one day and although it is different
every time I make it, it never fails."

Pil Pil Prawns

On holiday in southern Spain we sit for hours with family and friends over a table of food and Rioja. This recipe is a version of one of our Spanish favourites that I have adapted myself, having asked the waiter how it is cooked. So apologies to all the Spanish natives if it is not authentic!

 Serves 2  **Preparation time 5 mins** 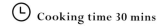 **Cooking time 30 mins**

Ingredients:

200mls olive oil

4 cloves of garlic

2 dried red chillies

1 tsp of "easy on the crushed chillies" from Waitrose

10-12 raw tiger prawns

Method

Pre-heat the oven to 180C.

Divide the olive oil between two individual ovenproof dishes, and warm through in the oven for 20 minutes. Whilst the oil is warming, chop the garlic and cut the chillies with scissors into several circular pieces, leaving out the seeds.

Once the oil is warmed through and sizzling, add the garlic, chillies and prawns to the hot dishes. Season to taste and add the teaspoon of crushed chillies (if you like it hotter) and return to the oven for 10 minutes, or until the prawns are cooked. Serve immediately with chunks of bread.

I bought some small ovenproof terracotta dishes in Spain which are ideal for this dish but have since discovered that they are readily available in department stores in the UK.

Niamh Kendall

Smoked Trout Pâté

A summery starter everyone likes. It can be served on starter plates or as canapés before sitting down.

 Serves 12 **Preparation time 15 mins**

Ingredients:

450g smoked trout flesh (must come from a trout farm or fishmonger, not the super market pre-packed stuff)

400g philadelphia cheese

1 tbsp crème fraîche

juice of one Lemon (add to taste)

1 dsp horseradish cream

lots of black pepper

chopped dill

Method

Pulse all the ingredients in a food processor until it forms a pâté (not too long!)

Chill before serving.

Serve with chopped dill on top, with fairy toast or ciabatta, or whatever takes your fancy.

Sarah Cameron

Fresh Mussels in a light Curried Coconut Sauce

This is a favourite in the Cookery School, Stirring Stuff. I can't remember how it came to be created, I imagine it was probably a store cupboard invention on an 'I can't really be bothered to cook' sort of night. We stir up this dish on the Fish and Shell fish course in the school and it has been known to appear on the Bistro Course too – Curry and Chips never tasted so good.

 Serves 4    **Preparation time 30 mins**   **Cooking time 15 mins**

Ingredients:

1kg fresh mussels – 1 bag

½ tsp fine oatmeal or polenta

1 tbsp light olive oil

1 small onion, finely diced

1 tsp mild madras curry powder

¼ tsp chilli powder

200mls fish stock or white wine

1x 450g tin chopped tomatoes

1 x 450g tin coconut milk

2 tbsp fresh coriander, chopped

Method

Put the fresh mussels into a large bowl and cover with cold tap water. Sprinkle ½ a teaspoon of very fine oatmeal or polenta over them and put them into the fridge for an hour. This will encourage the mussels to 'spit out' any grit.

When ready to cook, drain the mussels from the water and rinse well. Working under cold running water clean the mussels removing the beard and discarding any that are damaged or will not close.

Heat the olive oil in a large and lidded sauté pan. Add the diced onion and cook over a moderate heat until soft but not coloured. Add the spices and cook for a further 30 seconds or so or until aromatic.

Add the stock or wine, turn up the heat and bring to the boil. Add the mussels and cook with the lid on for 5 minutes or so until they are all well opened. Shake the pan occasionally to ensure even cooking.

Add the tomatoes and coconut milk and heat gently.

To serve, tip the mussels along with their sauce into a large serving bowl. Discard any that have not opened. Sprinkle with the chopped coriander and serve with lashings of fresh warm bread and a mixed salad.

Belinda Hill – Stirring Stuff Cookery School

Prawn and Mango Salad

I first came across this dish when a great friend gave it to us as a starter at a dinner party and I immediately asked for the recipe. It not only looks great and is very colourful, but the explosion of flavours and textures is really fresh and absolutely delicious. Although it does require a bit of putting together at the last minute, all the ingredients can be prepared in advance except for the prawns which take moments to cook. The finished product is definitely worth it. You'll really impress your friends with this one!

 Serves 4-6  **Preparation time 20 mins**

Ingredients:

Salad

4 tbsp ground nut oil

4 shallots, finely sliced

*king prawns (peeled), about
    5-6 per person or as
    you wish*

*2 medium ripe mangoes,
    peeled and sliced*

2 handfuls of coriander leaves

1 handful of mint leaves

*110g cashew nuts, toasted
    and chopped*

*1 red chilli, de-seeded and
    very thinly sliced*

Dressing

110mls rice vinegar

50g golden caster sugar

1 garlic clove, crushed

*1 small dried red chilli,
crushed or 1 tsp of crushed
    red chilli (available in jars
    in Waitrose)*

juice of 1 large lime

fish sauce to taste

Method

To make the dressing

Put the vinegar and sugar in a pan and bring it to the boil. Tip in the garlic and chilli and allow it to cool. Add the lime juice and a few drops of fish sauce. Set aside.

To make the salad

Heat the oil in a non-stick frying pan and fry the shallots until golden brown and crispy.

Arrange the herb leaves on 6 individual plates for serving, and put the mango slices on top.

Heat the frying pan up again and add the prawns to the shallots and cook until pink and cooked through. This should only take a few minutes.

To serve

On each plate put the prawns and shallots on top of the herb leaves and mango and scatter slices of the nuts and sliced chillies over the top. Spoon the dressing over everything.

Charlotte Tompkins

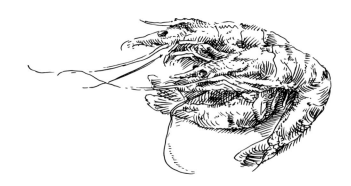

Ann's Thai Beef Salad

This tasty salad makes the ideal starter for a dinner party or a light lunch. I have made it a number of times and it was given to me by my good friend Ann.

 Serves 10  Preparation time 30 mins 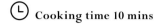 Cooking time 10 mins

Ingredients:

Salad

600g lean sirloin steak

1 bag mixed salad leaves
(110g)

1 bag bean sprouts (300g)

1 cucumber, peeled deseeded
and cut into match-sticks

a loose handful (roughly 20g)
each of coriander leaves,
mint and basil

5 spring onions, shredded

Dressing

5 tbsp lime juice – about
3 limes

4-5 tbsp Thai fish sauce

2 tbsp palm or soft
brown sugar

2 birds-eye chillies

Method

First make the dressing by mixing the lime juice, fish sauce and palm sugar. Stir until the sugar has dissolved. The dressing should have a sweet and sour taste, add more sugar or lime juice if needed but I would not add any more fish sauce. This can be stored in a jam jar until needed.

De-seed the chillies and dice them as finely as you possibly can. Put to one side until needed.

Season the steaks generously with ground pepper. Cook them individually on a very hot griddle or heavy based frying pan for about 2 – 2 ½ minutes each side. It is important not to overcook the steak, it should still be rare in the middle. Since you are eventually going to be cutting the steak into slices anyway, don't be frightened to cut a steak to test whether it is done. (Remember that the steak will carry on cooking even after you've removed it from the pan/griddle). Transfer onto a cooled plate and when the steaks have cooled somewhat cut into thin slices.

Mix the salad ingredients together in a large bowl and set aside.

When you are ready to serve, divide the salad onto 10 plates. Put the steak in a large bowl, toss with the dressing and chillies and spoon over the salad.

Sue Grundy

Chicken Livers with a sweet Spinach and Bacon Salad

This recipe is ideal as a starter or light lunch. The mincemeat is the kind we use for Christmas mince pies. Once puréed with the walnut oil, the spicy fruit flavour contrasts well with the peppery livers.

 Serves 4

Ingredients:

1 heaped tbsp mincemeat
4 tbsp walnut oil
8-12 chicken livers
4 rashers of streaky bacon
sea salt and pepper
olive oil
*12 handfuls of washed and
    ready-to-eat baby spinach*

Method

Put the mincemeat, walnut oil and 4 tablespoons of water into a food processor or blender and blitz to a smooth sauce, with dots of black raisin still visible.

Trim the chicken livers and place them on kitchen paper to dry.

Pre-heat the grill. Lay the bacon rashers on a grill tray with a rack, place under the grill, not too close to the top, and cook until crispy.

Season the livers with a good twist of pepper. Heat some olive oil in a non-stick frying pan and fry the livers for just a few minutes until golden brown on both sides. Season with a sprinkling of sea salt, remove from the pan and leave to rest.

Spoon some of the dressing on to the plates and scatter the spinach leaves and chicken livers onto it. Drizzle a little more dressing over the salad and top with a rasher of warm crispy bacon.

Gary Rhodes - Chef

"This recipe is ideal as a starter or light lunch."

Figs with Goats Cheese and Prosciutto

This really is simplicity itself but really delicious. Perfect for a summer starter or a light lunch.

 Serves 4   Preparation time 10 mins   Cooking time 10 mins

Ingredients:

4 figs

4 dsp soft goat cheese

4 slices prosciutto

1 tbsp runny honey

Method

Pre-heat the oven to 180C.

Make a deep cross into the top of each fig and gently prize open.

Carefully put a spoonful of goats cheese in the opening and wrap the fig with the prosciutto.

Place the figs on a baking tray and bake for 10 mins.

Serve on a bed of dressed salad leaves and drizzle with a little honey.

Penny Taylor

Figs with Goats Cheese and Prosciutto

Stuffed Mushrooms

This is a great recipe because it mixes the soft texture of the mushroom with the crunchy topping.
Fantastic served as a starter with a side salad or as an accompaniment to a juicy steak.

 Serves 4   Preparation time 20 mins   Cooking time 20 mins

Ingredients:

8 large portobello mushrooms

1 tbsp olive oil

50g butter

½ small onion, chopped finely

2 tbsp hazelnuts, chopped

1 clove of garlic, crushed

150g spinach

25g feta cheese, crumbled

25g cheddar cheese, grated

1 tbsp dill, chopped

salt and pepper

Method

Pre-heat the oven to 200C.

Remove the stems of the mushrooms and chop them roughly.

Heat the oil and butter in a frying pan and cook the onion until soft. Add the stems of the mushrooms, nuts and garlic and continue to cook for 1 minute.

Now add the spinach and cook for a few minutes until wilted.

Remove from the heat and stir in the feta and cheddar cheese together with the dill and seasoning.

Arrange the mushrooms cup side up in a baking dish.

Divide the stuffing between the mushrooms and bake for 10 minutes until slightly brown.

Serve warm with lightly dressed salad leaves.

Maria Fernandez de Pinedo

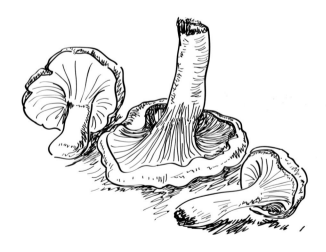

Baked Courgette and Aubergine Parmigiano

This gorgeous aubergine and courgette dish is one of my favourite veggie recipes and a longstanding favourite at both the London Street Brasserie and the Crooked Billet.

Courgettes are at their best when smaller, nutty and sweet. The big bloated ones, little Zeppelins, have a mushy texture and lack taste.

When I was a kid we had them sliced and boiled, pretty yuck. If cooking them as an accompanying vegetable, brush with olive oil, season and roast, grill, pan fry or barbecue, but don't boil them! Delicious simply sliced to thin ribbons and enjoyed raw, with a drizzle of olive oil, squeeze of lemon, salt and pepper.

Try baking courgette rings in a savoury custard. Whip up a couple of free-range eggs with 150mls full-fat milk, grated nutmeg, salt and pepper. Bake everything in an ovenproof dish for 30 mins.

 Serves 4-6  **Preparation time 20 mins**

Ingredients:

2 medium courgettes

1 large aubergine

2 free-range eggs, beaten

100g plain flour, seasoned

olive oil

200g tomato relish

2 buffalo mozzarella balls

75g shaved parmesan

maldon salt

freshly ground black pepper

Method

Pre-heat the oven 180C.

Slice the courgettes and aubergine lengthways, 4-5mm thick. Heat a ribbed griddle pan (or barbecue); brush courgette slices lightly with olive oil, season and grill – just 30 seconds a side to colour.

Heat a good centimetre of olive oil in a large frying pan. Dip the aubergine slices in seasoned flour, then into beaten egg, fry for 1 minute in the hot olive oil.

With tongs, turn the aubergine slices and fry until light golden for a further minute. Drain slices on kitchen paper.

Slice the mozzarella balls 4-5mm thick. Lay a fried aubergine slice on a baking sheet, spread with a 5mm layer of tomato relish. Lay a couple of courgette slices on top and put some shaved parmesan and sliced mozzarella on the courgette. Repeat the process again layering aubergine, tomato relish, courgette and finally a last generous layer of Parmesan and mozzarella.

The listed ingredients are sufficient for 2 parmigiano stacks.

Bake in a pre-heated 180C oven for 30 mins until the cheeses have melted and the tomato relish is bubbling.

Serve with roquette, basil, blushed tomato, olives and a little balsamic vinegar.

Paul Clerehugh - Chef

Fish

Easy Thai Prawn Stir Fry

This recipe is so quick and easy, my children love making it!

 Serves 4    **Preparation time 10 mins**   ⏲ **Cooking time 15 mins**

Ingredients:

2 tbsp sunflower oil

2 tbsp red or green Thai
curry paste

1 tbsp fish sauce

2 tbsp lime juice (approx
1 lime)

1 tsp sugar

200mls coconut milk

20 large raw prawns, shelled
and de-veined

1 large red onion, peeled
and sliced

200g asparagus, trimmed
and cut diagonally

1 red pepper, cored, de-seeded
and cut into thin strips

1 yellow pepper, cored,
de-seeded and cut into
thin strips

Method

Heat 1 tablespoon of oil in a wok or a large heavy based frying pan, add the prawns and stir fry for 2 minutes until pink.

Set aside.

Return the wok to a high heat and heat remaining oil, add the curry paste and cook stirring for 1 minute. Add the onion and asparagus and stir fry for 2 minutes. Now add the peppers and stir fry for a further 2 minutes. Add the coconut milk, lime juice, fish sauce and sugar and stir to combine together. Let this simmer gently for 3-5 minutes.

Finally add the prawns and heat thoroughly.

Serve with steamed rice or noodles.

Annette Miller

Easy Thai Prawn Stir Fry

Coconut Crab cakes with Mango Salsa

 Serves 2

Ingredients:

75g firm white fish fillet,
    such as cod, coley or
    haddock, skinned

2 tsp Thai fish sauce

2 birdseye chillies

1 garlic clove

200g white crabmeat, thawed
    if frozen, or canned

2 heaped tbsp coconut cream

2 spring onions

15g fresh coriander and basil

sunflower oil, for brushing

1 small ripe, firm mango

1 small red onion,
    finely chopped

1 lime

1 tsp white wine vinegar

2 tbsp light olive oil

50g bag ready to use
    watercress

salt and freshly ground
    black pepper

Method

Cut the white fish into chunks, making sure that there are no bones and place in a food processor. Chop up the chillies and garlic and add, then whiz for a few seconds to make a rough paste. Add the crabmeat and coconut cream and whiz again for a few seconds until just blended (you don't want to overdo it at this stage and lose the crab's texture). Scrape the mixture into a bowl.

Heat a flat griddle-pan. Finely chop the spring onions, coriander and basil and add them to the bowl, (reserving a heaped table-spoon of the herbs) stirring to combine. Season to taste. Using wet hands shape the mixture into 4 x 7.5cm / 3in patties and brush with the oil. Add to the pan and fry for 2-3 minutes on each side until lightly golden.

Slice the flesh away from each side of the mango's flat stone. Score the flesh into a small criss-cross pattern, turn out like a hedgehog and cut into a bowl. Add the reserved herbs, the onion, vinegar and olive oil. Squeeze in the lime juice and season to taste. Mix well.

Tip half of the salsa into the watercress and toss to combine.

Arrange the watercress mixture on a serving plate and spoon some more of the salsa into a small dipping plate and place on the side. Place two of the crab cakes on top and serve at once.

Ainsley Harriott - Chef

Salmon fishcakes with Chive Sauce

I am always on the lookout for a tasty dinner party dish that can be prepared in advance. This allows me to indulge in some chatter with my guests and the odd glass of vino rather than hiding in the kitchen amongst a plethora of steaming saucepans. This recipe really hits the mark and it also ticks another box with my non-meat eating wife! This very simple dish never fails to produce compliments and requests for the recipe.

 Serves 2   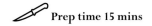 **Prep time 15 mins**   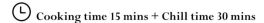 **Cooking time 15 mins + Chill time 30 mins**

Ingredients:

Fishcakes

350g cooked salmon

350g freshly cooked potatoes, mashed and cooled

1 tbsp tomato ketchup

1 tsp anchovy essence

2 tbsp fresh parsley, finely chopped

1 tbsp plain flour for dusting

1 tbsp olive oil

15g butter

Chive sauce

3 tbsp lemon juice

40g unsalted butter

125mls double cream

2 tbsp chives, finely chopped

Method

Pre-heat the oven to 200C.

Flake the salmon, removing all skin and bones. Mix half the salmon with the potato mash, ketchup, anchovy essence, and mix thoroughly. Season to taste.

Add the remaining salmon and parsley and mix in gently. This means there are some tasty salmon pieces in the cakes, not just a mush.

Divide the mixture into 4, lightly flour your hands and shape each piece into a deep fishcake. Place on a tray, cover with clingfilm and refrigerate for half an hour. For entertaining, this part can be done ahead of time.

Lightly flour the fishcakes. Heat a frying pan over a moderate heat, add the oil and then the butter. This will stop the butter browning and burning which can give a bitter flavour. When the butter starts foaming, add the fishcakes and fry for about 3 minutes until each side is browned.

Transfer to a baking dish and bake in the oven for 10-15 minutes until hot.

Make the sauce by heating the butter in a saucepan until it has just melted. Add the cream and heat through without boiling. Add the lemon juice and chives and warm through. Season with salt and pepper.

Serve with buttered spinach or leeks braised in stock and crushed new potatoes.

Tony Norman

My Mother-in-Law's Salmon Pasta

A very easy and impressive lunch if you are having people over. Very easy and quick to make and tastes delicious. Great with a nice cold glass of white wine.

 Serves 4   **Preparation time 15 mins**   **Cooking time 15 mins**

Ingredients:

300g penne pasta

225g smoked salmon

25g butter

1 onion, chopped

1 glove garlic, crushed

110g mushrooms, chopped

1 level tsp mild curry powder

1 level tbsp flour

150mls white wine

2 level tbsp crème fraîche

Method

Boil the water for the pasta whilst you are making the sauce. You can use any pasta for this, my favourite is penne or pasta twists.

Melt the butter in a large frying pan, add the chopped onion and fry until soft. Add the crushed garlic clove and mushrooms. Cook for 2-3 minutes. In a separate bowl mix the flour and curry powder together. Add this to the frying pan, stir in to soak up all the butter and juices.

Add the pasta to the boiling water and cook for 10-12 minutes.

Back to the sauce, gradually add the wine, stirring continuously. When all the wine has been added, cook for a further 3 minutes. Then add the crème fraîche.

Add the smoked salmon right at the last minute to the sauce, this literally needs warming through. You will know when it is ready when the salmon starts to change colour.

Drain the pasta after tasting to check it is ready. Serve the pasta with the sauce drizzled over the top.

Zoe Scott

"Great with a nice cold glass of white wine."

Farfalle al Salmone Gratinate

This is so easy and yet still full of flavour. A great mid-week recipe especially when time is short.

 Serves 6    Preparation time 25 mins   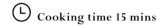 Cooking time 15 mins

Ingredients:

Pasta

350g farfalle pasta

80g salted butter, plus extra
 for greasing

200g smoked salmon, cut
 into small strips

3 tbsp fresh chives,
 finely chopped

100g parmesan cheese,
 freshly grated

salt and pepper to taste

Béchamel sauce

50g salted butter

50g plain flour

500mls cold full-fat milk

½ tsp paprika

pinch of freshly grated nutmeg

Method

Pre-heat the oven to 180C.

Cook the pasta in a large saucepan of boiling salted water until al dente.

Whilst the pasta is cooking, make the béchamel sauce. Melt the butter in a large saucepan over a medium heat. Stir in the flour and cook for 1 minute and then gradually whisk in the cold milk. Reduce the heat and cook for 10 minutes, whisking constantly. Once thickened, stir in the paprika and the nutmeg. Season and set aside to cool slightly. (The alternative cheat's method is to place all the sauce ingredients in the pan at the same time, whisking from the start until the sauce thickens!)

Drain the pasta and place in a large bowl with the butter, smoked salmon, chives, half the parmesan and half the béchamel sauce. Mix everything together.

Grease a 22cm round ovenproof dish with sides at least 4cm deep. Pour the pasta into the dish, cover with the remaining béchamel sauce and sprinkle over the remaining parmesan cheese. Place the dish in the pre-heated oven and cook for 15 minutes until golden and crispy.

Once ready, leave it to rest for 5 minutes. It will be easier to cut and serve as the layers will hold together. Serve with a lightly dressed green salad.

Gail Williams

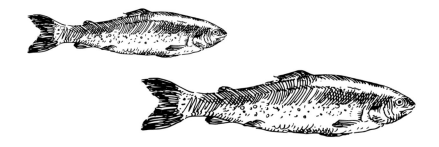

Chargrilled Salmon with Leek and Tarragon Sauce

This recipe has become a firm favourite for our bridge suppers. The ingredients are always close to hand, it's easy to make, and simply tastes delicious.

 Serves 2   Preparation time 15 mins   Cooking time 10 mins

Ingredients:

25g unsalted butter

2 medium leeks, washed
   trimmed and thinly sliced

150mls white wine

150mls whipping cream

1 tbsp tarragon roughly
   chopped

2 x 175g salmon fillets
   skin on

Method

Melt the butter in a medium-sized saucepan and add the leeks. Sweat the leeks for 5 minutes or until soft. Add the wine, bring to the boil and reduce by half. Add the cream and boil for 2 to 3 minutes. Season with salt and pepper. Finally add the tarragon leaves.

Pre-heat a cast iron grill pan or frying pan. Brush the salmon with a little oil then season with salt and pepper. Place the fillets on the grill pan flesh side down and cook for 5 to 6 minutes. Turn over and cook for a further 2 to 3 minutes.

Re-heat the sauce, pour it on to a plate and top with the salmon fillets.

The sauce can be made in advance and gently reheated. It is also a great partner to chicken, turkey or a white meaty fish like hake.

Mary Bullock

Chargrilled Salmon with Leek and Tarragon Sauce

Wild Salmon Trout with Asparagus, Peas and a Citrus Butter Vinaigrette

👪 Serves 4   🔪 Preparation time 30 mins-1hr   🕐 Cooking time 10-30 mins

Ingredients:

Fish

1 large fillet of wild salmon
   trout, about 500g

2 tbsp light olive oil

8 asparagus spears, peeled
   and chopped into
   1cm pieces

125g shelled fresh peas

1 leek, sliced into 1cm slices

handful pea shoots (optional)

salt and freshly ground
   white pepper

Citrus butter vinaigrette

2 tbsp finely chopped shallots

150mls dry white wine

1 tsp grated lemon zest

150g unsalted butter

salt and freshly ground
   black pepper

Method

Check the fish for bones, removing any you find, and carefully scale the skin side with a blunt serrated knife. Rinse and pat dry. Cut into four portions and carefully make four or five shallow incisions in the skin of each portion using a very sharp knife. Brush liberally with light olive oil and set aside.

To make the vinaigrette, boil the shallots with the white wine in a small saucepan until reduced by half. Add the lemon zest and allow to infuse while you clarify the butter.

Melt the butter in another saucepan and bring to a gentle boil for 3-4 minutes. Remove from the heat and allow to settle, then skim off any foam or scum from the top. Pour the clear butter into the shallot reduction, leaving any milky residue behind in the pan (discard the milky residue). Season the vinaigrette with salt and freshly ground black pepper and set aside. Warm through for serving.

Season the salmon trout fillets with salt and freshly ground white pepper and fry skin-side down in a hot pan. Cook until the skin is nicely crisp and the fish is just cooked. This should take 5-8 minutes, depending on the thickness of the fillets.

While the fish is cooking, cook the asparagus, peas and leeks in a pan of boiling salted water until just tender. Drain thoroughly.

To serve, scatter the pea shoots (if using) in with the hot vegetables and spoon into the centre of each warmed plate. Spoon over the warm butter vinaigrette, and top with the fillets of fish.

Paul Rankin - Chef

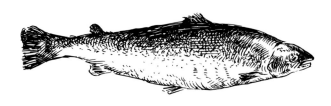

Salmon Pie with Capers, Black olives and Pine nuts

I have a recollection that this recipe was hauled from a magazine by a brilliant cooking friend of mine at least 17 years ago. The truth is that I have cooked it so often I mentally consider it to be mine, so if anyone out there claims it, I do apologise. It is the perfect prepare ahead lunch or supper and needs nothing more than a green salad, although you can add new potatoes if you are hungry. A fresh out of the oven delicious puff pastry vision.

 Serves 6 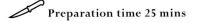 **Preparation time 25 mins** **Cooking time 25 mins**

Ingredients:

1kg skinless salmon fillet

110g black olives, cut up a bit

1 bunch spring onions,
*   finely sliced*

150g toasted pine nuts

100g melted butter

2½ tbsp capers

zest of 1 orange and 1 lemon

1 pinch of cayenne pepper

2 packets of puff pastry

Method

Pre-heat the oven to 200C.

Cut the salmon into large cubes. Mix together the salmon, olives, spring onions, pine nuts, melted butter, capers, orange and lemon zest and cayenne pepper. Season with salt and pepper.

Roll out the pastry into two circles large enough for the base and top of a 25cm flan ring. Line the flan ring generously with larger circle of pastry allowing it to fall over the sides a bit. Fill with the salmon mixture. Lay the last pastry circle on top, trim and decorate. Brush with beaten egg. Bake in the oven for about 25 minutes or until golden.

Fiona Mates

Smoked Salmon, Rocket and Chilli Tarts

This is my favourite standby for unexpected guests, fab with a simple salad and a glass of wine. The filling can be changed depending on what you have in your fridge and the pastry works!

 Serves 8　 Preparation time 20 mins　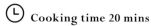 Cooking time 20 mins

Ingredients:

Pastry (or packet of short crust)

175g flour

75g butter

1 egg

1 tbsp water

Filling

1 red chilli, chopped

150g smoked salmon, chopped

large handful of rocket, chopped

200mls double cream

2 eggs

Method

Pre-heat the oven to 200C.

Use either two 4 portion Yorkshire pudding trays, 8 - 10 cm tart tins, or a quiche tin. Place a baking sheet on the bottom shelf of the oven.

To make the pastry, measure flour and butter into a food processor and whiz until it resembles fine breadcrumbs. Add the egg and water and whiz again until combined to a dough ball. Chill for an hour if time allows, if not roll out thinly and line the pastry tins. Chill (again).

To make the filling

Heat a knob of butter in a non-stick frying pan and add the chilli until softened. Allow to cool.

Spoon out the chilli between the pastry cases. Sprinkle over the smoked salmon and the chopped rocket.

Whisk the eggs and cream, season, and pour over the tart bases.

Place on baking sheet (to allow pastry to cook) and bake for about 20 minutes until golden brown.

Eva Davies

Salmon Filo Parcels

This dish has become a favourite of mine since I lost weight. Surprisingly it is a weight watchers recipe that I have adapted to suit me!! I have made it for every occasion and it is always a big hit. Best served with lots of steamed green vegetables and a chilled glass of white wine.

 Serves 4  Preparation time 1 hr  Cooking time 25 mins

Ingredients:

4 salmon steaks (4cm x 15cm
    in length)

8 sheets of filo pastry

4 tbsp philadelphia
    full fat soft cheese

1 large red pepper, de-seeded,
    sliced thinly

2 courgettes, thinly sliced

1 red onion, peeled and
    thinly sliced

1 tbsp olive oil

salt and pepper

milk for glazing

Method

Pre-heat oven to 180C.

Prepare the vegetables and place on a baking tray, sprinkle with salt, pepper and olive oil, toss everything around in the oil to get a good coating. Place on the highest shelf of the oven for 30-40 minutes or until the vegetables are toasted brown at the edges. Allow to cool.

Meanwhile place two sheets of filo pastry on the worktop, placing a salmon steak in the middle. Spoon 1 tablespoon of the cheese on to the salmon and spread. Divide the roasted vegetables into 4 and put one portion on top of the cheese. Carefully wrap the filo pastry around the salmon and filling to form a tight parcel. (Top tip - be careful not to slit the pastry!!) Glaze with some milk.

Repeat for each of the 4 salmon fillets.

Place on a baking tray and bake on the middle shelf of the oven for 20-25 minutes until golden brown.

Sarah Ingram

Thai Red Salmon Curry

Although I am not the greatest fan of salmon, I appreciate that it offers great health benefits so I concocted this recipe through trial and error, using our favourite Asian flavours and spices! It really is a cross between a Thai and Chinese stir-fry and is now one of our regular everyday suppers! The curry paste can be made in advance so it is also a great recipe for entertaining.

 Serves 6    **Preparation time 30 mins**   **Cooking time 15-20 mins**

Ingredients:

Thai red curry paste

1 red onion, quartered

2 red chillies

4 cloves of garlic

2 cms ginger

½ tbsp of cumin

1 tsp of ground coriander

¼ tsp of white pepper

2 tbsp of soy sauce

1 or 2 tsp of chilli powder

80mls coconut milk (taken from 400mls tin to be used later)

juice of ½ lime

½ tsp cinnamon

Curry

1 tbsp olive oil

6 fillets of salmon, cubed

200g french beans

1 large broccoli, cut into small florets

2 red peppers, diced

2 courgettes, cut into batons

320mls of coconut milk

Method

To make the Thai curry paste, place all the ingredients in a food processor and blitz until smooth.

To make the curry, heat the oil in a heavy-based saucepan or wok. Stir fry the vegetables on a high heat for 1-2 minutes.
Add the salmon cubes and turn down the heat. Cook for 2 more minutes. Add the red curry paste and the coconut milk. Stir in. Put a lid on and simmer for 5-7 minutes to cook the salmon.

Serve on its own or with rice, topped with a fresh sprig of coriander!

The Thai curry paste can be made in advance and stored in a jar in the fridge.

Simon Bullock

Butternut Squash, Salmon and Prawn Curry

This became an instant hit with the "Cooking with Love" committee. We had it at one of our early dinner meetings and everyone begged for the recipe.

 Serves 6    Preparation time 20 mins   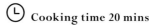 Cooking time 20 mins

Ingredients:

1-2 tbsp red Thai curry paste
(according to taste)

400mls coconut milk

350mls fish stock

3 tbsp fish sauce

2 tbsp caster sugar

3 lemongrass stalks cut in half
and bashed with a knife

3 lime leaves cut into strips
(can be omitted)

½ tsp turmeric powder

1kg butternut squash peeled
and cut into large cubes

500g salmon fillet, skinned
and cut into large cubes

500g peeled raw prawns

pak choi, shredded

½ a lime juiced

small bunch of coriander
to serve

Method

Heat a large saucepan or casserole dish. Add the curry paste with a small amount of coconut milk. Cook over a medium heat stirring all the time. Add the rest of the coconut milk, fish stock, fish sauce, sugar, lemongrass, lime leaves and turmeric. Bring to the boil.

Add the butternut squash and simmer until tender (about 10 minutes).

Add the salmon and prawns and boil for 3-4 minutes until cooked. Add the pak choi and once it has wilted, add the lime juice. Season with salt and pepper. Sprinkle with coriander just before serving.

Serve with Thai or Basmati rice.

Nicky Blystad

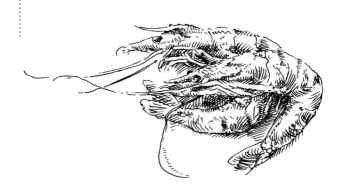

Salt Baked Fish

This is a local dish in Southern Spain and the fish is usually the catch of the day from the Straits of Gibraltar. The waiter really "wowed" me when this arrived on a trolley especially for me. He placed a large napkin over the salt baked fish and with two spoons carefully removed the top crust of salt to reveal the fish, which was then plated for me. The salt is a clever way to easily remove the fish skin and the fish remains moist and therefore does not require a sauce. Goes well with a green salad or plate of simple vegetables. Any white fish can be used, sea bass, sea bream...

 Serves 2    Preparation time 10 mins   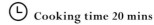 Cooking time 20 mins

Ingredients:

1.5kg of (Maldon) sea salt

2 egg whites beaten until firm

1 sheet of greaseproof paper

sea bream / sea bass fillet
    or whole as preferred.

Method

Pre-heat the oven to 180C.

Whisk the egg whites with an electric whisk until it forms soft peaks. Add the sea salt to the bowl and stir until blended.

Take an oven tray, place the greaseproof paper on the bottom, and spread it with enough of the salt mixture to coat one side of the fish. Place the prepared fish on the salt and cover with the rest of the mix.

Bake at 180C for 20 minutes (it will continue to cook happily for another ten minutes)

Break the crust of the baked sea salt using a napkin and the back of a spoon in front of guests and serve immediately on a warmed plate. The fish skin should come away with the salt, leaving the fish easy to remove from the salt bake.

Niamh Kendall

Fish Crumble Bake

This is a great family supper dish - quick, delicious and best of all it has converted my teenage son into a fan of fish, so it's now a regular favourite in our house. If you don't have time to make the topping, you can always use a jar of good quality red pesto but making your own only takes a couple of minutes in the food processor.

 Serves 6    **Preparation time 10 mins**   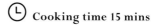 **Cooking time 15 mins**

Ingredients:

*600g cod, halibut or
    salmon fillet*

1 tbsp olive oil

*200g coarse breadcrumbs
    (from a crusty loaf)*

2 cloves garlic

6 anchovy fillets in oil

140g sun dried tomatoes in oil

handful of fresh basil

40g parmesan

1 lemon

1 tbsp balsamic vinegar

Method

Pre-heat the oven to 180C.

Season the fish with salt and pepper, rub in the olive oil and place the fillets on a baking sheet. Bake in the oven for 5 minutes.

Put the peeled garlic cloves, anchovy fillets, sun dried tomatoes with a bit of their oil, Parmesan, grated zest plus the juice of the lemon, balsamic vinegar and basil leaves into the food processor and blend to a paste. Add the breadcrumbs and mix together on the pulse setting of the processor.

Remove fish from oven and spread the bread paste over the fish fillets. Return to oven and bake for a further 10 minutes until the topping is crisp and golden.

Serve with crushed new potatoes and a green salad.

Lisa Gordon

Easy Fish Stew

This stew tastes authentic despite taking such a short time to make. Other seafood can be added, such as scallops or squid, and I often serve a bowl of aioli with the stew for added depth.

 Serves 8    **Preparation time 10 mins**   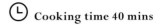 **Cooking time 40 mins**

Ingredients:

5 tbsp olive oil

3 garlic cloves, crushed

2 onions, chopped

2 leeks, trimmed and sliced

2 celery stalks, sliced

1 fennel bulb, trimmed
   and sliced

1 tbsp plain flour

1 bay leaf

a sprig of thyme

a generous pinch of saffron

3 cans chopped tomatoes,
   410g each

2 litres fish stock

1kg monkfish tail, cut into 8

500g mussels, scrubbed

8 scallops

8 uncooked prawns, shell on

a bunch of flat leaf
   parsley, chopped

salt and pepper

Method

Heat the olive oil in a large pan and add garlic, onions, leeks, celery and fennel. Cook gently for 10 minutes, until soft.

Sprinkle in the flour and stir well. Add the bay, thyme, saffron, tomatoes, fish stock and seasoning. Bring to the boil, and simmer for 25 minutes.

Add the monkfish, mussels, prawns and scallops, cover and simmer very gently for 6 minutes. Remove from heat and leave with the lid still on for 4 minutes.

Add parsley and serve with lots of bread.

Kate Sloane

Fabulous Fish Pie

For ladies that lunch or for a hearty supper for the family, this is always my fool-proof tasty recipe.

 Serves 6    Preparation time 50 mins   Cooking time 30 mins

Ingredients:

5 large potatoes

salt and ground black pepper

2 free range eggs

2 large handfuls of fresh
    spinach

1 onion finely chopped

1 carrot, halved and
    finely chopped

1 tbsp olive oil

300mls of double cream

2 good handfuls of grated
    mature cheddar or
    parmesan cheese

1 lemon, juiced

1 heaped tsp english mustard

1 large handful of flat-leaf
    parsley, finely chopped

400g skinless haddock or
    cod fillet, diced

100g prawns

Method

Pre-heat the oven to 230C.

Boil the potatoes in a large pan of salted water. At the same time, hard-boil the eggs. Steam the spinach until wilted and squeeze out the excess moisture and put to one side.

In a separate pan, heat the olive oil and slowly fry the onion and carrot for about 5 minutes. Add the double cream and heat through without boiling. Remove from heat. Add the cheese, lemon juice, mustard and parsley.

Put the spinach, fish, prawns and eggs into an earthenware dish and mix together. Then pour over the cream and vegetable mixture. Mix roughly together.

Mash the potatoes with a little olive oil, salt and pepper and put it over the fish mixture, don't worry about making it look pretty it's a homely, hearty thing.

Bake in the oven for 25-30 minutes.

Serve with green beans lightly cooked and mixed with olive oil and some fine raw garlic and salt. It tastes great with this.

Nikki Derbyshire

Creamy Tomato Fish Curry

This is a lovely, mild cream fish curry whose star ingredients are lovely sweet sour tomatoes and of course, the fish. This dish is easy enough to cook for a delicious mid-week meal but equally delicious and elegant enough to impress your friends. You can use any fish you like, I like to use fish steaks in most of my curries but monkfish also works really well. I like to fry my fish steaks before adding it to the sauce but you don't have to, especially if you use firm white fleshed fish fillets like monkfish. This is lovely with a pilaf or with Indian flat breads.

 Serves 4   **Cooking time 30-35 mins**

Ingredients:

500-550g firm white fish
  steaks, such as halibut,
  halved or even monkfish
  (don't fry monkfish, add
  straight in)

7 tbsp vegetable oil

1 small onion, finely chopped

6 fat garlic cloves, peeled

10g ginger, peeled weight

1 tsp turmeric

¼- ½ tsp red chilli powder

1 tbsp coriander powder

4 medium tomatoes, quartered
  and de-seeded

500mls water

salt and freshly ground black
  pepper to taste

¾ tsp garam masala

2 tbsp single cream

handful of fresh coriander
  leaves to garnish

Whole spices

2 bay leaves

6 cloves

6 green cardamom pods

12 black peppercorns

Method

Rub ½ teaspoon of the turmeric and a good pinch of salt into the fish and leave to marinate as you cook the sauce.

Heat 5 tablespoons of the oil in a medium-sized non-stick sauce-pan. Add all the spices and once they have sizzled for 10 seconds, add the onions and cook until golden brown.

Meanwhile, blend the tomatoes, ginger and garlic until smooth. Add this paste to the pan with the spices and salt. Cook over a moderate-high flame, stirring often until the masala releases oil droplets, around 10-12 minutes. Turn the heat down and "brown" the paste for a further 6 minutes to intensify the flavours. Add the water and bring to a boil, simmer for 6-7 minutes. Taste and adjust the seasoning.

Meanwhile fry the fish. Heat the remaining oil in a frying until very hot. Add the marinated pieces of fish and cook, undisturbed for 2 minutes. Turn over and cook this side until golden brown, another 2 minutes or so.

Taste and adjust the seasoning of the sauce and add the fried fish, garam masala and cream to the curry. Simmer for another 3 minutes so the sauce thickens. Taste and adjust seasoning and serve.

Anjum Anand - Chef

Pan Fried Monkfish with Mustard Dill Sauce on Crushed New Potatoes with Watercress

For all those amateur cooks who, like me, invite friends round and then panic over what to rustle up, this simple yet impressive and totally delicious dish is a guaranteed winner. They'll think you're straight off Masterchef! The key is not to overcook the fish.

 Serves 4  **Preparation time 40 mins**

Ingredients:

Fish

500g monkfish tails – ask
    your fishmonger to remove
    the skin, bone and
    membrane

2 tbsp good quality olive oil

sea salt

Sauce

black pepper

2 shallots, finely chopped

1 clove garlic, finely chopped

1 tbsp good quality olive oil

3 tbsp white wine

100mls double cream

3 tbsp coarse grain mustard

2 tbsp chopped dill plus
    extra for serving

Potatoes

750g small new potatoes
    scraped clean

50g watercress sprigs
    roughly chopped

2 tbsp good quality olive oil

Method

Cut the fish into medallions about 2.5cm thick. Season with a little sea salt and black pepper and place in the refrigerator.

Cook the potatoes in salted water until tender. Drain and reserve.

To make the sauce heat the oil in a heavy-based frying pan, add the shallots and garlic and fry gently for about 3 minutes or until soft. Add the wine and cook until evaporated. Stir in the cream and bring gently to the boil. Add the mustard and dill, season to taste and set aside to keep warm.

Now for the fish, wipe the pan with kitchen paper and heat the oil until very hot. Add the monkfish medallions and cook for about 2 minutes on each side until slightly browned and just firm when pressed. Remove and drain on kitchen paper. Keep warm.

Heat the remaining oil in the same pan and add the potatoes gently crushing each one against the side of the pan until it bursts open. Season with salt and pepper and add the watercress turning gently until it is wilted and well mixed in.

To serve, place the potatoes in the centre of each plate with the monkfish medallions on top. Pour over the sauce and garnish with a little chopped dill.

Steve Knott

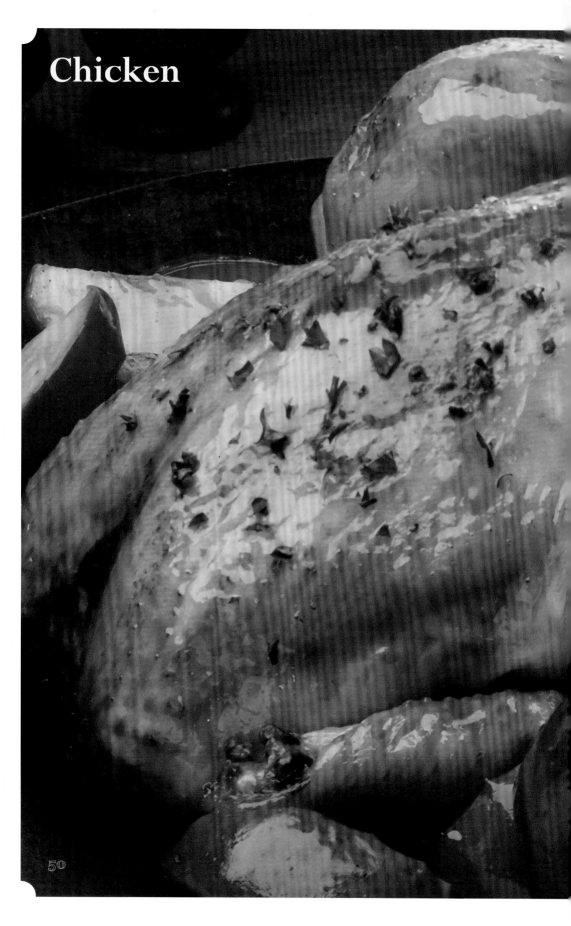

Chicken

My Mother's Coronation Chicken

The awful truth is that I do not cook much now, in many ways I wish I did, but when I did cook this was invariably on the summer menu.

 Serves 6    Preparation time 20 mins   Cooking time 2 hrs

Ingredients:

1 medium chicken

butter

salt

1 tbsp olive oil

1 tbsp curry powder

60mls chicken stock

1 tsp tomato purée

lemon juice

2 tbsp apricot jam

1 large onion

150mls mayonnaise

3 tbsp single cream

Method

Roast the chicken in butter and salt.

Heat the oil in a saucepan and add the chopped onion. Fry gently until soft but not brown. Stir in the curry powder. Add the stock, tomato purée, lemon juice and jam. Continue to stir until boiling. Simmer for 5 minutes and liquidise thoroughly. Cool.

Add the mayonnaise and cream. Mix properly, and taste continually when you're doing this bit, to get it just right.

Finally, pour the sauce over the cooked, cold chicken.
Sprinkle with almonds (if you like them).

There are different ways of serving it. I like hot new potatoes with butter and mint, and a salad, or maybe just watercress. It isn't at all difficult but it tastes as if it were.

Julian Fellowes - Actor, Novelist and Screenwriter

Chicken and Parma Ham Salad

This dish represents summer lunches for my three daughters, one of the few things that they agree on!

 Serves 8  **Preparation time 20 mins** ◷ **Cooking time 25 mins**

Ingredients:

Salad

8 chicken breasts, skinned
  and boned

1 x 100g pack Parma ham,
  cut into strips

100g packet pine kernels,
  toasted

1 x 285g jar of sun dried
  tomatoes, drained and
  sliced.

basil, for garnish

Dressing

1½ tbsp of balsamic vinegar

6 tbsp oil from the sundried
  tomatoes jar

tsp dijon mustard

salt and pepper

Method

Preheat the oven to 180C.

Brush the chicken fillets with oil and place in one layer on a baking sheet. Bake for 20-25 minutes until cooked, do not over cook. They should be springy to the touch. Leave to cool.

Combine all the ingredients for the dressing in a jug and whisk together.

Slice the chicken thinly and put in a bowl, add the ham and sun dried tomatoes. Dress and gently mix. Turn out onto wide, shallow serving dish. Scatter the pine nuts and basil over the top.

Kate Sloane

Chicken and Parma Ham Salad

Curried Turkey Salad with Dried Fruits

I found this recipe in a magazine about 10 years ago. The page is now so stained and faded it is barely legible and the reason I kept it was actually for the Onion Tart on the adjacent page, a recipe to this day I've never attempted! It has stood me in good stead when feeding a crowd, is always popular and is good in summer with other salads or in winter with jacket potatoes. It tastes even better the next day so don't be afraid to make it well ahead of time. Oh, and most importantly of all, it is idiot-proof!

 Serves 10-12   **Preparation time 15 mins**

Ingredients:

900g cooked turkey or chicken (or 2 medium ready-cooked chickens)

1 tbsp madras curry paste

75g raisins

75g dried apricots, quartered

75g whole blanched almonds

150mls mayonnaise

75mls natural yogurt

2 tbsp mango chutney

1 bunch spring onions, chopped, incl. the green parts

150g baby leaf salad

1 tbsp fresh coriander leaves

salt and pepper

Method

Pre-heat the oven to 180°C.

Spread the almonds out on a baking tray and roast them in the oven for 8 minutes, using a timer so they don't burn! Leave them to cool for a couple of minutes, then roughly chop them.

Cut the turkey or chicken into bite-sized pieces and place in a large bowl.

Mix the mayonnaise, yoghurt, mango chutney (cut up any large pieces of mango) and curry paste and pour this over the meat. Add the raisins, apricots, three-quarters of the spring onions and two-thirds of the almonds. Mix everything together, season, cover and chill until needed.

When you're ready to serve, place the salad leaves in the base of a large serving dish and spoon the turkey or chicken on top. Scatter over the remaining spring onions, almonds and all the coriander.

Sarah Tipple

Thai Chicken Noodle Salad

This simple recipe originally came from a daily newspaper and is one that gets churned out repeatedly, especially for "girls' lunches", and I get asked for the recipe every single time. It has certainly done the rounds now and it's one of those simple (once you have all the ingredients!), sure-fire successes that always goes down well. The flavours in it are amazing.

 Serves 4    Preparation time 30 mins

Ingredients:

Dressing

1 tbsp sesame oil

3 tbsp soy sauce

lime juice

2 tbsp rice wine vinegar

1 tbsp brown sugar

2 red chillies, finely chopped

1 tsp Thai fish sauce
   (optional)

Salad

1 barbecued chicken

110g mangetout, topped
   and tailed

1 bag prepared bitter
   leaf salad

½ bunch spring onions

½ cucumber, finely chopped

55g dry roasted peanuts,
   roughly chopped

2 tbsp coriander leaves

1 tbsp freshly chopped mint

2 tbsp sesame seeds,
   lightly toasted

250g egg rice noodles

Method

Make the dressing by whisking all the ingredients together.

Remove the flesh from the chicken, discarding the skin. Shred into thin slices.

Cook the mangetout in boiling salted water for 2-3 minutes. Rinse under cold water and drain very well.

Cook the noodles according to the instructions on the packet, drain and cool.

Toss the salad leaves, spring onions, mangetout, cucumber, chicken, peanuts, coriander and mint leaves together with the salad dressing. Sprinkle with the toasted sesame seeds and serve immediately.

Lucy Montgomery

Quick Chicken Curry and Spicy Salad

This tasty curry is quick and easy to prepare. It is served in pitta bread pockets so makes a great lunchtime meal to be enjoyed by all the family!

 Serves 2 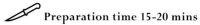 **Preparation time 15-20 mins** **Cooking time 10-15 mins**

Ingredients:

Chicken curry

3 tbsp olive oil

1 medium onion, peeled
    and sliced

400g chicken breasts, diced

2 cloves garlic, crushed

1 green chilli, de-seeded
    and finely chopped

¼ tsp salt

¼ tsp turmeric

½ tsp ground cumin

¼ tsp ground coriander

1 tsp tomato purée

¼ tsp garam masala or
    1 tsp curry paste

2 tbsp double cream

pitta bread

Spicy salad

1 tbsp olive oil

¼ tsp black pepper

½ green chilli, de-seeded and
    finely chopped (optional)

pinch of salt (optional)

½ tsp runny honey

1 tbsp balsamic, cider,
    wine or malt vinegar

1 packet mixed green
    salad leaves

Method

Heat the oil in a frying pan, and fry the onion for 1 minute. Add the chicken and continue to fry for 5-6 minutes. Stir in the garlic and chilli and continue to cook, stirring from time to time.

Whilst the mixture is browning, make up the salad dressing by placing all the ingredients in a clean jar with a lid and shake well.

Now add the salt, turmeric, cumin and coriander to the chicken mixture, continuing to stir.

Add the tomato purée and garam masala, then fold in the cream.

To serve, dress the salad leaves with the spicy dressing and serve the curry on the side. Alternatively push everything into warmed pitta bread pockets.

Stephen and Emma Bullock

Nikki's Creamy Chicken Curry

Don't be put off by the long list of ingredients, this is a really easy curry to make and you'll have all the spices already in your store cupboard! The intensity of the curry can be altered by adding more or less madras curry powder. For a tomato flavour, add half a can of chopped tomatoes and reduce the amount of chicken stock.

 Serves 4    **Preparation time 20 mins**   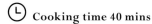 **Cooking time 40 mins**

Ingredients:

1 tbsp olive oil

1 tbsp mustard seeds

1 large onion, chopped

3 cloves garlic, crushed

4 chicken breasts, diced

½ tsp turmeric

2½ tsp medium madras curry powder

1 tsp chilli powder

2 tsp paprika

1 tbsp wine vinegar

1½ tbsp soy sauce

275mls chicken stock

2 tbsp lemon juice (approx 1 lemon)

150mls single cream (alternatively use crème fraîche or natural yogurt)

Method

Heat the oil in a heavy-based saucepan on a moderate heat and add the mustard seeds for a couple of minutes, until they start to 'pop'. Add the onion and cook until soft and pale gold. Increase the heat slightly and add the garlic and cook for a further 2 minutes. Add the diced chicken, and a little more oil if required, and stir fry for 2-4 minutes, until golden. Add the spices, wine vinegar, soy sauce, chicken stock and lemon juice and stir until thoroughly mixed.

Turn the heat right down, put the lid on the pan and let it cook gently for about 35-40 minutes, stirring from time to time.

Just before serving, stir in the cream and serve with rice or naan bread and a green salad.

Nikki Derbyshire

Thai Chicken with Chilli Jam

This is a family favourite that I get asked to cook again and again...who says mid-week recipes are boring?
Try it with a simple rocket salad and some warm bread. Easy, quick and delicious!

 Serves 8 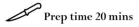 **Prep time 20 mins** **Marinating time 1 hr + Cooking time 50 mins**

Ingredients:

8 boneless chicken breasts

Marinade

4 tbsp sesame oil

4 tbsp Thai fish sauce

1 tbsp clear honey

3 garlic cloves, chopped

2 red chillies, de-seeded
    and finely chopped

25g fresh coriander, finely
    chopped

Chilli jam

500g ripe tomatoes, chopped

4 red chillies, de-seeded
    and chopped

4 garlic cloves

5cm piece of fresh root
    ginger, chopped

2 tbsp Thai fish sauce

300g soft brown sugar

100mls red wine vinegar

3 Thai lime leaves

55g raisins

Method

Mix the marinade ingredients together in a bowl. Slice the chicken into strips and place in the marinade. Put in the fridge for 1 hour or overnight.

To make the chilli jam, blend half the tomatoes with the chilli, garlic, ginger and fish sauce in a liquidiser or food processor until smooth. Transfer to a heavy-based saucepan, add the sugar, vinegar, lime leaves and raisins. Slowly bring to the boil, stirring all the time.

Dice the remaining tomatoes and add to the jam. Simmer gently for 45 minutes, stirring occasionally until the jam thickens. Leave to cool.

Pre-heat a large griddle, frying pan or barbecue. Cook the chicken for 5 minutes on each side, basting it with the marinade as it cooks.

Serve hot or cold with the chilli jam.

Maria Fernandez de Pinedo

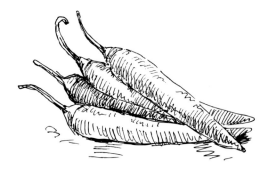

Chicken Satay

When our children were young, we lived in Jakarta. Chicken Satay is a popular street food and is cooked on barbecues on practically every street corner. It was our youngest son, Stuart's favourite food and he used to eat it nearly every day for lunch at his nursery school. I just had to get the recipe to bring home. The secret ingredient is the sweet soy sauce (ketchap manis) and it definitely makes all the difference.

Serves 4   **Prep time 10 mins**   **Marinating time 30 mins + Cooking time 15 mins**

Ingredients:

Satay

1 clove garlic

2cms ginger, finely chopped

juice of a lemon

1 tbsp oil

450g chicken, cubed

2 large tbsp sweet soy sauce
*   (ketchap manis)**

pepper

Satay sauce

2 tsp brown sugar

250g peanuts

1 garlic clove

juice of a lemon

salt and pepper

200mls coconut milk

Method

To make the satay, mix all ingredients in a bowl and leave in the fridge to marinate for 30 mins.

Thread the chicken onto skewers and cook in a hot pan, under the grill or on a barbecue, turning regularly. Baste with the marinade while cooking. Be careful not to burn.

To make the satay sauce, crush the peanuts and fry in garlic and oil. Place in a liquidizer or food processor with the lemon juice, sugar, salt and pepper and blend to a rough paste, gradually add the coconut milk and blend again until the sauce is a suitable consistency for dipping. Return to the frying pan and cook for a further few minutes.

Serve in a dish alongside the satay.

*Ketchap manis is available from several supermarkets, but dark soy sauce can be substituted

Mary Smith

Rose Harissa Chicken

This is a really impressive chicken dish for easy lunchtime entertaining or a light supper. Serving the chicken on a bed of green beans and flageolet beans really gives this dish the wow factor.

 Serves 6    Preparation time 25 mins   Cooking time 15 mins

Ingredients:

2 tsp cumin seeds

2 tsp coriander seeds

6 chicken breast fillets

4 tbsp olive oil

1 tsp belazu rose harissa

4 tbsp sweet balsamic and red pepper dressing (Waitrose)

300g cherry vine tomatoes

Method

Crush the cumin and coriander seeds using a pestle and mortar. Season with a little salt.

Slice each chicken breast horizontally into 2 thin slices. Rub the spice mix over all the slices.

Heat 3 tbsp of the oil in a large frying pan and fry the chicken slices a few at a time until thoroughly cooked. Place on a plate and keep warm.

To make the dressing, add the remaining oil to the pan with the rose harissa, the balsamic and red pepper dressing and 4 tbsp of cold water. Bring to the boil and stir in the tomatoes and cook for 1-2 minutes until heated through.

Serve on a bed of lightly cooked green beans and canned flageolet beans. Spoon the tomatoes over and drizzle with the dressing.

Maria Lockhart

Chicken with Chorizo

This is a lovely quick easy dish that works equally well as a delicious supper or alternative Sunday roast.

 Serves 6   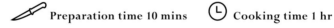 Preparation time 10 mins   Cooking time 1 hr

Ingredients:

2 tbsp olive oil

12 chicken thighs, bone in, skin on

750g chorizo sausages cut into 4cm chunks

1kg new potatoes, halved

2 red onions, peeled and chopped into segments

½ jar sundried tomatoes, drained

2 tsp dried oregano

1 orange, grated zest

Method

Pre-heat the oven to 160C.

You will need two shallow roasting tins. Put one tablespoon of the oil and six chicken thighs into each tin. Turn the chicken thighs in the oil to coat and place them skin-side up.

Add the chorizo sausages, sundried tomatoes, onion segments and the new potatoes to both tins in between the chicken pieces. Sprinkle the oregano and then the grated orange zest over the contents of both tins.

Cook in the oven for 1 hour, after 30 minutes swap the top tray with the bottom tray and baste. Serve with a fresh green salad or a bowl of steaming hot green vegetables.

Lizzie Yell

Chicken Crème Fraîche with Chorizo Sausage and Roasted Cherry Tomatoes

This delicious recipe was handed down by a French au pair and I have adapted it to cook in my Aga. I can leave it cooking slowly in the simmering oven without it drying out and it really develops the tasty flavours. It can equally be cooked in a conventional oven and is served best on a bed of brown rice with lots of green vegetables and some roasted cherry tomatoes.

 Serves 4 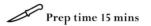 Prep time 15 mins 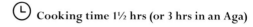 Cooking time 1½ hrs (or 3 hrs in an Aga)

Ingredients:

Chicken

30mls olive oil

4 chicken breasts – cut into chunks

500g tub of full fat crème fraîche

150g chorizo sausage – skinned and cut into 1cm slices

125mls of dry white wine

30mls of olive oil

salt and pepper

Roasted cherry tomatoes

12 ripe cherry tomatoes – cut in half

2 cloves of garlic – crushed

5g mixed herbs

15mls olive oil

Method

Pre-heat the oven to 150C.

Heat the oil in a casserole dish and, when it is fairly hot, add the chicken pieces. Brown them to a nutty golden colour, add the chorizo sausage and sauté until the sausage has taken on some colour.

Add the white wine and crème fraîche and as soon as everything has reached a simmering point, put a lid on the casserole and transfer it to the middle shelf of the pre-heated oven for 1½ hours or until the meat is tender. Season to taste before serving.

To make the roasted tomatoes, place the tomatoes on a baking tray and sprinkle with the herbs, garlic, and oil. Place on the top shelf of the oven and roast for 40-45 minutes or until golden and crispy.

Sarah Ingram

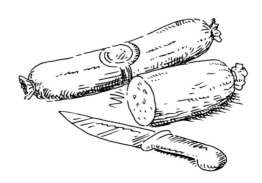

Milan Chicken

The stuffing in this recipe gives an Italian twist to roasting chicken breasts. It's very easy to make and looks very impressive, so perfect for entertaining.

 Serves 6    **Preparation time 20 mins**   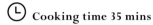 **Cooking time 35 mins**

Ingredients:

Chicken

15g butter

6 chicken breast or supremes, with skin on

seasoning

2 tbsp runny honey

200mls crème fraîche

2 tbsp pesto

300g cherry vine tomatoes

Stuffing

50g butter

1 medium onion, finely chopped

3 slices Parma ham, snipped into small pieces

40g fresh white breadcrumbs

50g parmesan cheese, grated

4 tbsp chopped parsley

1 egg, beaten

Method

Pre-heat the oven to 200C.

To make the stuffing, heat the butter in a heavy-based frying pan and fry the onion for 2 minutes. Cover, lower the heat, and cook for about 10 minutes until the onion is soft and pale gold. Add the ham, increasing the heat, and fry for 2 minutes to crisp. Place in a mixing bowl to cool.

Add the breadcrumbs, Parmesan, parsley and egg to the mixing bowl, mixing thoroughly and seasoning well.

Loosen the skin from the chicken breast/supreme, leaving one side attached to make a small pocket. Divide the stuffing into 6 and stuff into the pocket of each piece of chicken. Stretch back the skin to cover the stuffing.

Place the chicken pieces in a buttered roasting tin and brush the skin with a little runny honey and bake in the oven for 20-25 minutes, until the chicken is cooked and golden.

Place the tomatoes on a baking tray and cook in the oven for the same time as the chicken. Transfer the chicken and tomatoes to a warm plate to rest.

Now make the sauce. Add the crème fraîche to the juices left in the tin, scraping the bottom of the tin so all the juices and flavours are combined. Whisk over a high heat and then stir in the pesto to warm through.

To serve the chicken, top with the roasted cherry tomatoes and drizzle over the sauce. Green beans and roast potatoes are a great accompaniment.

Maria Wilson

Chicken with Pesto and Feta Cheese

A quick and easy chicken dish that can be served hot or cold.

 Serves 4   Preparation time 10 mins   Cooking time 30 mins

Ingredients:

4 chicken breasts

1 jar of pesto (200g approx)

1 pack of feta cheese (200g)

parmesan cheese

olive oil

Method

Pre-heat the oven to 220C.

Mash the feta with a fork and mix to a mush with the pesto and a tablespoon of olive oil.

Bash the chicken breasts stuff with the Feta mixture and, fold over to make a parcel. Arrange in an oven-proof dish with a drizzle of olive oil and parmesan grated over the top.

Bake in the oven for half an hour. The parmesan should be crispy on top.

Elizabeth Reid

Milan Chicken

Chicken Earle

I developed 'Chicken Earle' with my cookery teacher, Mrs. Earle when I was 16. I took it home and it was a big hit with my whole family, so I kept making it and then so did my mum and because we didn't know what else to call it, we named it after my teacher! Sadly, I never got the chance to tell her about this before she died but her name lives on and has been shared many times over with all my family and friends!

 Serves 4    **Preparation time 20 mins**   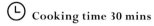 **Cooking time 30 mins**

Ingredients:

Chicken

4 chicken breasts, cut into
    mouth-size pieces

4 rashers of bacon or
    pancetta, chopped

1 onion, chopped

½ leek, chopped

2 garlic cloves, crushed

2 tbsp plain flour

seasoning

2 bay leaves

2 tbsp olive oil

275mls chicken stock

275mls milk

mushrooms (optional)

Topping

50g fresh breadcrumbs

50g grated cheddar cheese

Method

Pre-heat the oven to 200C.

Sauté the chicken pieces in olive oil for 3-4 minutes on a high heat and remove from the pan to a plate.

Gently fry the onion, leek and bacon for approximately 5 minutes or so. Add the garlic and return the chicken to the pan and continue to fry for another minute. Add the flour and salt and pepper and stir around for a minute for the flour to cook. Slowly add the chicken stock and bay leaves, stirring well as you add, it should slowly thicken. Add the milk and taste for seasoning. Add halved or quartered mushrooms if using. Transfer to an entrée dish or shallow casserole.

Mix the fresh breadcrumbs with the grated cheese and sprinkle on top of the chicken mixture, covering to form a crumble-style topping.

Bake in the oven for 30 minutes until the top is crispy and the sauce is bubbling up a little at the edges.

Anne Keeling

Boursin Chicken

Having enjoyed pork stroganoff for many years, I developed this recipe as an alternative under the careful eye of Jane, my 'cook-extraordinaire wife'. I then went "off piste" with the addition of Boursin and from there, gradually refined the recipe to our liking. It really is essential to 'just' cook the chicken to ensure the meat is tender and flavoursome.

 Serves 4    **Preparation time 25 mins**   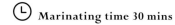 **Marinating time 30 mins**

Ingredients:

1 large white onion, sliced/diced

225g button mushrooms

2 garlic cloves, crushed

4 boneless, skinless breasts

1 tsp of vegetable stock powder

1 Boursin cheese 150g (peppered version optional)

250mls double cream

250mls white wine

2 tbsp of olive oil

25g unsalted butter

Method

Chop each chicken breast into bite-sized pieces. Marinate the chicken in the white wine, half the crushed garlic and olive oil. Add a good pinch of salt and pepper and leave for 30 mins.

In a pan, fry the onion and remaining half of the garlic together in olive oil and butter until soft and golden. Add the mushrooms and cook for another 2 minutes. Remove from pan.

Re-heat the pan and sear the chicken quickly until cooked on all sides. Add the reserved onion and mushrooms to the chicken and mix together. Add the remaining marinade liquid. Sprinkle the stock powder over all the ingredients and cook for one more minute. Place the Boursin cheese in the centre of the pan and allow to melt down. Stir in the cream. Do not allow to boil. Continue stirring until the chicken is cooked. If too thick add a little milk (or wine!)

Serve with rice or new potatoes .

John Barnard

Chicken with Sundried Tomatoes, Tarragon and Lemon

A quick and easy chicken dish, great for a mid-week supper.

 **Serves 6**   **Prep time 20 mins**   **Marinating time 30 mins + Cooking time 5 mins**

Ingredients:

5/6 chicken breasts - skin off,
    sliced thinly

8 tbsp fresh lemon juice

2 heaped tsp smoked
    sweet paprika

½ clove, crushed

1 tbsp chopped fresh tarragon

14 sundried tomatoes, sliced

275mls double cream

salt and pepper

Method

Combine the chicken, lemon juice, paprika, garlic and tarragon in a bowl, and put in the fridge to marinate for at least 30 minutes or overnight.

Heat a little oil in a frying pan, add a knob of butter, let it foam but not brown, and then add few strips of chicken at a time and brown on both sides. Transfer the chicken to a casserole dish.

Add the cream to the chicken juices in the frying pan to deglaze. Keep stirring and bring the cream to the boil, allow the sauce to thicken for couple of minutes then add to the chicken in the casserole dish. Add the sundried tomatoes and cook for a further 5 minutes. Check seasoning as it will need little salt and black pepper.

Fee Turner

Chicken Corine

This recipe is originally from Belgium and I have cooked this dish since the 1980's. It makes a great supper with lots of flavour and a hint of spice, and is a complete meal in itself. You can also substitute cooked chicken, so is a great way to use leftovers.

 Serves 6    **Preparation time 40 mins**   **Cooking time 25 mins**

Ingredients:

6 streaky bacon rashers, diced

50g butter

3 boneless chicken breasts
   cut into strips

2 medium onions,
   thinly sliced

2 large green peppers,
   de-seeded and coarsely
   chopped

225g button mushrooms,
   halved

275g long grain rice, washed
   and soaked in cold water
   for 30 mins

5 medium sized tomatoes,
   blanched, peeled and
   coarsely chopped

275g can sweetcorn

½ tsp dried thyme

1 tsp salt

½ tsp black pepper

¼ tsp celery salt

¼ tsp cayenne pepper

2 tsp Worcestershire sauce

400mls chicken stock

50g parmesan cheese

Method

In a medium-sized flameproof casserole, fry the bacon over a moderate heat for 5 minutes or until crisp and golden. Remove from the casserole and drain on kitchen paper towels. Set aside on a large plate.

Add half the butter to the casserole. When the foam subsides, add the chicken strips and fry, stirring frequently for 6-8 minutes or until the chicken is lightly browned. Remove from the casserole and set aside with the bacon.

Add the onions and peppers to the casserole, fry for 5 minutes, stirring frequently. Add the mushrooms and fry for a further 3 minutes. Remove from the casserole and set aside with the chicken and bacon.

Add the remaining butter to the casserole. When the foam subsides, add the drained rice. Fry for 3 minutes, stirring constantly.

Stir in the chicken, bacon, vegetables, tomatoes, sweetcorn, thyme, salt, pepper, celery salt, cayenne, and Worcestershire sauce. Stir well to mix. Add the chicken stock. Bring to the boil, stirring constantly. Reduce the heat to very low, cover the pan and simmer for 20 – 25 minutes or until the rice is cooked and has absorbed all the liquid.

Remove from the heat. Pile onto a warm serving dish and sprinkle over the Parmesan cheese. Serve immediately.

Hazel Hawkes

Lemon, Pancetta and Thyme Roasted Chicken

 Serves 4    Preparation time 10 mins   Cooking time 1 hr 10 mins

Ingredients:

1.5kg chicken

125g softened unsalted butter

1 tbsp fresh chopped thyme

150g chopped pancetta

1 lemon, zested and juiced

200g green beans

Method

Pre-heat the oven to 190C.

Mix together the softened butter, thyme, pancetta, lemon zest and juice.

Loosen the skin at the top of the crown of the chicken and push the index and middle fingers underneath to form a pocket. Score the thighs twice on both sides.

Push ¾ of the butter mix into the pocket under the skin and rub the remaining mix into the thighs of the chicken.

Cover with foil and roast for 40 minutes.

Remove from the oven, remove the foil and baste the chicken with the juices. Return to the oven uncovered and cook for a further 30 minutes, basting occasionally. Remove from the oven and allow to rest.

Boil the beans in salted water for 2-3 minutes. Carve the chicken.

Arrange the carved chicken on warmed serving plates and drizzle over some of the cooking juices. Serve with green beans and a spoonful of warmed mashed potato.

James Tanner - Chef

Connie's Chicken Dish

Adapted from a recipe created in wartime Britain by my grandmother's best friend who was married to an accountant and never wasted anything - the recipe is great, a bit different and can easily be doubled to feed many hungry mouths!

 Serves 6    Preparation time 15 mins   Cooking time 30 mins

Ingredients:

1 large cooked chicken or turkey (great for using left-overs)

1 large can of cream of chicken soup

110g chopped celery

2 tbsp finely chopped onion

50g chopped almonds

salt and pepper

1 tbsp lemon juice

3 hardboiled eggs, cut into chunks

20g mayonnaise or salad cream

Method

Pre-heat the oven to 190C.

Mix all the ingredients together in a greased casserole dish and bake for about 30 mins.

The dish can be covered with potato crisps just before serving.

Stella McDonough

Chicken in the Orchard Pie

Terrific for an Autumn night. My tired and hungry boys loved coming back on their exeat weekends and tucking into this pie. Pop it in the oven and watch it disappear.

 Serves 6  **Preparation time 20 mins**  **Cooking time 45 mins - 1 hr**

Ingredients:

25g butter

700g chicken breast, diced

1 tbsp flour

300mls cider

3 tsp dried tarragon

1 tsp Dijon mustard

150mls single cream

1 apple, peeled and sliced

100g mushrooms, sliced

seasoning

1 packet puff pastry

1 egg, beaten

Method

Pre-heat the oven to 200C.

Melt the butter in a heavy-based frying pan and add the chicken to seal and brown on a moderate heat. Stir in the flour to absorb all the meat juices. Slowly add the cider, stirring gently. Now add the tarragon and mustard and continue cooking for another few minutes.

Add the cream, apple, mushrooms and seasoning and cook for a further 15 minutes.

Transfer to a pie dish and cover with the puff pastry. Make a small slit in the pastry for the steam to escape. Brush with the beaten egg and cook for 15-20 minutes until golden.

Serve with mashed potatoes and green vegetables.

Marilyn Withnell

Tagliatelle with Chicken Livers in Tomato Sauce

The first time we enjoyed this scrummy 'taste of Italy', was when we holidayed on the west coast of Scotland. It was cooked for us by a dear friend, making a long lunch with the odd glass of chianti. Afterwards we went out in small boats, in the sunshine, to empty lobster pots...it was all heaven!

 Serves 4    **Preparation time 20 mins**   **Cooking time 10 mins**

Ingredients:

300g of chicken livers

6 tbsp of olive oil

1 large onion, peeled and
   finely sliced

4 bay leaves

big pinch of nutmeg to taste

3 tbsp dry sherry

2 tbsp tomato purée

2 tbsp of chicken stock

170mls sour cream

salt

freshly ground black pepper

450g fresh tagliatelle

75g freshly grated
   pecorino cheese

2 tbsp flat leaf parsley
   chopped

2 tbsp toasted pine nuts

Method

Cut the chicken livers into small slices.

Heat the oil in a frying pan and cook the onion very gently for 5 minutes. Add the chicken livers and bay leaves, and fry gently for 6 minutes over a low heat. Add the nutmeg and sherry, and cook for 1-2 minutes. Stir in the tomato purée, and enough stock to make a smooth sauce. Add salt and pepper to taste.

Cook the pasta for 3-5 minutes or until al dente. Drain and mix with the sauce.

Serve sprinkled with pine nuts, pecorino cheese and some chopped flat leaf parsley.

Harriet Wynn Jones

Venison, Cranberry and Port Casserole

Such an easy dish, a glorified stew which is a winter special served with mashed potato, red cabbage and carrots. Suits all ages taste-wise which is why it's become tradition for me to serve it every Boxing Day, making and freezing it in advance!

 Serves 6    **Preparation time 20 mins**   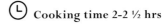 **Cooking time 2-2 ½ hrs**

Ingredients:

olive oil

1.35kg venison, trimmed
    and diced

200g smoked lardons

2 tbsp plain flour

4 tbsp tomato purée

300mls Port

450mls beef stock

400g tin of plum tomatoes

310g pot of cranberry sauce

300g shallots, peeled

300g fresh cranberries

black pepper

Method

Pre-heat the oven to 160C.

Heat the oil in a heavy based frying pan and brown the diced venison in small batches. Put to one side.

Fry the lardons and once brown, return the venison to the pan. Stir in the plain flour which will soak up all the meat juices and then stir in the tomato purée. Add the Port slowly whilst stirring gently and cook for 2 minutes. Now add the beef stock slowly, stirring all the time until the sauce is a good consistency. Add the plum tomatoes, cranberry sauce, shallots and season with ground black pepper and bring the casserole to simmering point.

Transfer to a casserole dish and place in the pre-heated oven for 1 ½ -2 hours, stirring every now and again.

Half an hour before serving, add the fresh cranberries and return to the oven for the final cooking time.

Serve with mashed potatoes, carrots and red cabbage.

Liz Huysinga

Game Casserole

A wonderful, rich winter casserole that is great for entertaining or cooking for the family. Serve as a casserole or as individual pies, topped with puff pastry.

 Serves 8  **Preparation time 20 mins** 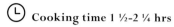 **Cooking time 1 ½-2 ¼ hrs**

Ingredients:

1.4kg mixed game meats (duck and pheasant work really well)

2 tbsp sunflower oil

75g butter

200g smoked streaky bacon

4 leeks, thickly sliced on the diagonal

50g plain flour

300mls red wine

600mls chicken stock

4 tbsp redcurrant jelly

salt and fresh ground pepper

2 large oranges (1 for garnish)

2 tbsp chopped fresh parsley

Method

Pre-heat the oven to 160C.

Trim the meats and cut into 5cm pieces.

Heat the oil and half the butter in a large non-stick frying pan or casserole, and cook the game and bacon over a high heat until sealed and brown. You will have to do this in batches. Add a little more oil if necessary. (Don't be tempted to put too much meat in the pan at once as it won't seal or brown properly). Remove with a slotted spoon and set aside.

Add the remaining butter to the frying pan and add the leeks and fry over a high heat for a few minutes.

Sprinkle in the flour and gradually blend in the red wine, stock and redcurrant jelly. Bring to the boil, stirring all the time. Season with salt and pepper.

Transfer the leeks and sauce into a casserole. Then add the whole orange and meats. Cover and put in the oven for 1 ½ - 2 ¼ hours or until the meats are tender. (The cooking time will vary depending on the variety of meats used: venison for example, tends to take a little longer to become really tender). Check the liquid halfway through cooking, adding a little more stock if necessary.

Once the game is tender, lift the softened orange into a sieve, cut in half, stand over a bowl and push the orange through the sieve, collecting the juice. Gradually stir the juice into the casserole until the taste is perfect.

Check the seasoning and add a little more stock if the casserole is still a little thick.

Garnish with freshly chopped parsley and orange slices. Serve with mashed potato and fresh vegetables – red cabbage goes particularly well.

Jill Hatton

Normandy Pheasant with Apple Rings

This dish has been a favourite of mine for many years. Apples are of course, top of the list of ingredients in Normandy cooking, hence the origins of this recipe. It doesn't have to be seasonal as the pheasant breasts freeze well. Over the years we have enjoyed this with family and friends alike and I hope you will too.

 Serves 6-8    **Preparation time 40 mins**   **Cooking time 1 ½-2 hrs**

Ingredients:

Pheasant

30g butter

1 tbsp sunflower oil

2 pheasants cut into portions

*2 cooking apples, cored,
    sliced and quartered*

2 celery stalks, sliced

1 onion sliced

1 tbsp plain flour

300mls game stock

150mls dry white wine

salt and black pepper

150mls double cream

chopped parsley as garnish

Apple rings

*2 cooking apples, cored
    and sliced into 5mm rings*

30g butter

caster sugar

Method

Pre-heat the oven to 180C.

Melt the butter with the oil in a flameproof casserole dish. When the butter is foaming, add the pheasant pieces and cook until they are brown (about five minutes). Lift out of the pan and drain.

Lower the heat, add the apples, celery and onion and cook until soft (about 5-6 minutes). Add the flour and stir whilst cooking for 1 minute. Pour in the stock and wine, add salt and pepper to taste, and bring to the boil, stirring until lightly thickened.

Return the pheasant to the casserole. Bring back to the boil, cover with greaseproof paper and the casserole lid and cook in a pre-heated oven for 1 to 1 ½ hours until tender.

Remove the pheasant from the casserole with a slotted spoon, place on a warmed plate and keep warm.

Strain the sauce into a saucepan. Whisk in the cream, taste for seasoning and re-heat gently.

To make the apple rings, melt the butter in a frying pan and add the apple rings. Sprinkle a little caster sugar over the top of the apple. Cook over a high heat, turning once, for 3 minutes or until the sugar has caramelised and the apples have turned golden brown. Remove from the pan and keep warm.

Place the pheasant on serving plates with the apple rings. Spoon the sauce over the pheasant and serve immediately with garnish.

A wonderful way to enjoy moist, delicious pheasant.

Joyce Lockhart

Pheasant with Mango Chutney and Cream

This is a quick and easy but delicious way of cooking pheasant breasts and it could be used for other game or chicken as well.

 Serves 6  Preparation time 20 mins Cooking time 10-15 mins

Ingredients:

1 large onion, finely chopped

1 tbsp olive oil

6 pheasant breasts

425mls double cream

3 tbsp mango chutney

3 tbsp Worcestershire sauce

salt and pepper

Method

Pre-heat the oven to 200C.

Heat the oil in a frying pan and gently cook the onion. Set aside.

Season the pheasant breasts and brown quickly in hot oil.

In a bowl, stir the mango chutney and Worcestershire sauce into the double cream.

Layer the onions into an ovenproof dish and place the pheasant breast on top. Pour over the cream mixture and dust with paprika (optional).

Cook in the oven for 10-15 minutes. It is important not to overcook the pheasant breasts as they will become tough and stringy. As I have an AGA I cook mine for about 30-45 minutes in the simmering oven as then they cook very slowly and stay moist.

Bridget Lanyon

Seared Duck Breasts with Soy and Ginger

This is one of my favourite dinner party dishes. It is easy, very tasty and can be prepared ahead.
It evokes memories of evenings round the dinner table with good vibes and delicious red wine.

 Serves 8  **Preparation time 10 mins** **Cooking time 30 mins**

Ingredients:

8 duck breasts

couple of pinches of each - salt,
    black and cayenne pepper

500mls chicken stock

8 tbsp soy sauce

8 tbsp rice wine (or white wine)

4 tbsp grated fresh ginger root

4 tsp tomato purée

couple of pinches of chilli
    powder (to taste)

4 tbsp lime juice

Method

Pre-heat oven to 200C.

Use a sharp knife to score across the duck breasts 4 times through the skin and fat, but just barely to the meat. Rub the skin with salt, cayenne and black pepper.

Pre-heat an oven-proof griddle pan over a medium-high heat. Lay the breasts, skin side down in the pan and fry until the skin is brown and crisp (approx 5 minutes, depending on size). Turn the breasts and cook for a further minute.

Place the pan in the pre-heated oven and roast the breasts for approx 5-8 minutes, depending on how you like them served, ideally they should be pink. Set aside in a warm place to rest (can be covered with aluminium foil). This can be done in advance of guests arriving if necessary.

Place the stock, soy sauce, rice wine, ginger, tomato purée, chilli powder and lime juice in a saucepan, bring to the boil and simmer for approx 2 minutes to thicken slightly.

Slice the duck breasts thinly and arrange on warm serving plates, pour a little of the sauce over, and put the rest in a jug to be handed round the guests.

Delicious served with roast new potatoes and green beans.

Nicky Blystad

Seared Duck Breasts with Soy and Ginger

Braised Duck with Peas

 Serves 4   Preparation time 30 mins   Cooking time 1 ½ hrs

Ingredients:

2 x 1kg ducks

75g butter

225g bacon

175g small button onions

570mls duck stock

1 tbsp chopped sage

1 tbsp chopped mint

1 tbsp chopped parsley

450g frozen peas

1 head of lettuce (round)

salt and pepper

Method

Pre-heat the oven to 160C.

Put the giblets into the stock and leave to gently simmer for 30 minutes.

Cut the bacon into thick lardons i.e. 1 cm squares. Melt 25g butter and add the lardons. Add the button onions and gently colour along with the lardons. When nicely coloured take out and keep on one side.

Prick the ducks all over and rub with a little salt. Colour in the same pan as the lardons and onions and take out of pan. Drain off all fat and put ducks back in the pan.

Strain the stock into the pan and bring to the boil and cover with a lid. Put in oven and cook for 1 hour.

Add the button onions and lardons and braise for a further 15 minutes.

Take the ducks out and allow to rest, keep warm. Remove excess fat.

Shred the lettuce into strips add the sauce with the peas and the herbs. Reduce this sauce by 1/3 to correct the consistency, and season. Monte au beurre with 50g butter (add small chunk of the butter one at a time, whisking until melted, to give the sauce a velvety texture and rich flavour).

Carve the ducks and put on a flat plate. Pour sauce over and serve.

Brian Turner – Chef

Meat

Asian Beef with Vegetables

This is a great favourite with my two boys. I always think you can tell the success of a recipe by the splash and smear marks on the page… 10 years after first cooking this dish the recipe is well thumbed, smeared and splattered!

 Serves 4 Prep time 25-30 mins ⏱ Marinating time 20 mins + Cooking time 15 mins

Ingredients:

Marinade

1 tbsp soy sauce

1 tbsp sake or sherry

1 tsp sesame oil

1 tsp cornflour

**Beef, vegetables
    and pasta**

225g beef fillet, rump
    or sirloin cut into strips

175g pasta twists

3 tbsp sunflower oil

1 clove of garlic

1 onion, thinly sliced

100g carrots, sliced

100g French beans, topped
    and tailed

100g red pepper, sliced
    lengthways

salt and pepper

Sauce

½ chicken stock cube
    in 90mls water

6 tbsp boiling water

½ tsp rice wine vinegar

1 tsp soy sauce

1 tsp sugar

½ tsp cornflour

Method

Mix together the marinade in a bowl and add the strips of beef. Marinate for 20 minutes.

Steam the carrots and beans for about 5 minutes until tender and set aside.

Cook the pasta according to the instructions on the packet, drain and keep warm.

Mix together the ingredients for the sauce.

Heat 1 tbsp oil in a frying pan, add the beef and cook for 3 minutes. Remove the meat and add the remaining oil to the pan. Fry the onions and garlic for 3 minutes. Add the pepper and cook for 2 minutes. Add the carrots, beans and beef, season with salt and pepper then stir in the sauce and the cooked pasta to warm through.

Tessa Rose

Barbecued Pork Chops

Our summer barbecues have always included barbecued pork, either as spare ribs or pork chops. Although these are cooked in the oven and not on the barbecue, they are such a family favourite that we never have a barbecue without them.

 Serves 4    **Preparation time 20 mins**   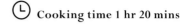 **Cooking time 1 hr 20 mins**

Ingredients:

2 tbsp vegetable oil

1 tbsp butter

4 pork loin chops

150mls tomato purée

1 onion, finely chopped

2 celery stalks, chopped

150mls red wine

juice of a lemon

1 tbsp brown sugar

1 tsp prepared mustard

½ tsp salt

¼ tsp black pepper

Method

Pre-heat the oven to 180C.

Heat the butter and oil in a large heavy-based frying pan, or skillet. Add the pork chops and brown on both sides. Remove from the pan and place in a shallow oven-proof dish.

In a small bowl, combine the rest of the ingredients. Pour over the pork chops. Cover the dish with foil and bake in the centre of the oven for 40 minutes, basting occasionally.

After 40 minutes remove the foil and cook for another 40 minutes uncovered.

Neil Hawkes

Beef in Beer with Dumplings

Growing up in a large family in the 60s and 70s, I have many happy memories of steaming casseroles and mountains of mashed potatoes. Our favourite was always the casseroles topped with soft dumplings, there could never be enough!! This 'grown up' version of the recipe has become a firm family favourite for a new generation!

 Serves 4    **Preparation time 20 mins**   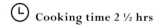 **Cooking time 2 ½ hrs**

Ingredients:

Beef

olive oil

2 medium onions

600g braising steak

1 fat garlic clove

1 bottle beer (330mls)

25g plain flour

125mls water

1 tsp dried thyme

1 tsp Dijon mustard

splash Worcestershire sauce

salt and pepper

Dumplings

50g vegetable suet

100g self-raising flour

seasoning

water

Method

Pre heat the oven to 150C.

Cut the onions into wedges and gently heat in the oil in a large casserole pan until soft, approximately 10 minutes. Add the garlic and cook for another minute.

Meanwhile, cut the braising steak into largish pieces and brown off in a frying pan.

Add the browned meat with all the juices to the casserole with the onion and garlic. Sprinkle in the flour and give it a good stir over a moderate heat. Add the beer and water but don't worry if it looks lumpy at this stage, just continue to stir. Add the thyme, mustard, Worcestershire sauce and seasoning. Put the lid on the casserole and put in the oven for 2 hours. After an hour, give it another stir and add more liquid if necessary.

Meanwhile make the dumplings by mixing the suet, flour and seasoning. Add sufficient water to make a dough consistency.

After 2 hours cooking, ensure there is plenty of liquid in the casserole as the dumplings will absorb some of this liquid. Increase the oven temperature to 180C. Spoon the dumplings into the casserole, return the lid and put in the oven for a further 30 minutes.

Maria Lockhart

Beef Rendang

This is a traditional West Sumatran dish known as Minangkabau or "Victorious Buffalo" but is also excellent with beef if buffalo is not available at your local butcher.

 Serves 8    **Preparation time 10 mins**   **Cooking time 2-3 hrs**

Ingredients:

1½kg of brisket or stewing steak

6 shallots

3 cloves of garlic

salt

1 tsp of ground ginger

1 tsp of turmeric

3 tsp chilli powder

½ tsp galingale (or fresh ginger)

7½ cups coconut milk

1 bay leaf

1 fresh turmeric leaf
(optional)

Method

Cut the meat into biggish cubes.

Crush the shallots and garlic with some salt. Add the ginger, turmeric, chilli and galingale (or fresh ginger). Mix them together and put into a basin with the coconut milk. Add the meat and the various leaves.

Cook slowly in a large heavy saucepan, letting the mixture bubble gently and stirring occasionally until it becomes very thick. This should take 1½-2 hours. Add salt if necessary.

When the mixture is thick, the slow cooking must continue, but now the meat and sauce must be stirred occasionally until all the sauce has been absorbed by the meat and the meat itself becomes golden brown. This will take at least half an hour, sometime as much as 1½ hours.

Serve with plain rice.

Nick Bullock

Beef with Passion Fruit

 Serves 2

Ingredients:

250g lean beef fillet

2 tbsp oyster sauce

1 tsp cornflour

½ tsp black pepper

1 ½ tsp brown sugar

2 cloves garlic

4 whole passion fruit

4 sprigs coriander

2 tbsp oil

4 thin slices ginger

4 tbsp white wine

Method

Slice the beef thinly across the grain.

In a large bowl, mix the oyster sauce, cornflour, black pepper and sugar. Toss the beef in this mixture to season it.

Chop the garlic.

Peel the passion fruit and cut into four pieces.

Chop the coriander and spring onions for garnishing.

Heat the oil in a wok or frying pan and stir fry the garlic and ginger until aromatic. Increase the heat to high, add the beef and stir fry for five minutes. Stir in the wine and passion fruit to warm through.

Garnish with the chopped coriander and spring onions.

Nancy Lam - Chef

Chickpea and Chorizo Stew

This is delicious and so simple to create. It takes me to a place I love to be....sitting in the shade of the Pepper tree in the hot Spanish sun, naturally with a beautiful glass of Rioja to hand. I can almost hear those cicadas ringing in my ears.

 Serves 4    **Preparation time 15 mins**   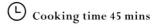 **Cooking time 45 mins**

Ingredients:

2-3 tbsp olive oil

2 large onions, chopped

4 cloves garlic, thinly sliced

4 chorizo sausages

1 tsp crushed dried chillies

a glass of dry white wine

5 or 6 tomatoes

2 x 400g tins chick peas

1 dsp brown sugar

1 tbsp flat leafed
    parsley, chopped

Method

Heat the olive oil in a deep, heavy-based pan or casserole. Add the onions, stirring to coat them, and then let them cook at a moderate heat. Stir in the garlic and leave to cook, partially covered by a lid, until the onions are soft and pale gold.

Cut each sausage into about 4 fat chunks. Mix these in with the softened onions then add a tsp of the dried crushed chillies. Pour in a glass of white wine and bring it to a fast bubble.

Chop the tomatoes roughly, add them to the casserole and bring to the boil. Add the drained and rinsed chick peas, and a can of water. Season with salt and black pepper. Stir in the dessert spoon of brown sugar. Bring to the boil then turn down to a simmer and leave to cook slowly, half covered with a lid for 45 minutes.

Give it a stir from time to time and check the consistency. You want to end up with a rich, brick-red sauce with a spiciness from the chillies and chorizo.

Just before serving, stir in the roughly chopped parsley. Serve in shallow bowls, making sure everyone gets their fair share of chorizo.

Serve with plenty of crusty bread to soak up the juices, and a lovely green salad.

Lindsay Metcalf

Fruity Beef Casserole

If "not another casserole" is a regular moan in your house, then try this variation on beef casserole.
The plum jam and chilli turn this from an everyday meal into something much more luscious. It is
guaranteed to convert even the die hard anti-casserole out there.

 Serves 4 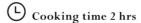 Preparation time 20 mins  Cooking time 2 hrs

Ingredients:

olive oil

1kg stewing beef, diced

2 medium onions,
 thinly sliced

2 carrots, peeled and sliced

1 fat garlic clove, crushed

1 heaped tbsp tomato purée

1 heaped tbsp plain flour

½ tsp chilli powder

1 lemon, zested plus
 1 tbsp juice

500mls beef stock

150g plum or damson jam

Method

Pre-heat the oven to 160C.

Heat the oil in a large casserole dish and brown the stewing beef in small batches, setting aside as you go along. Rest the browned beef on a plate.

Now, add the onion to the casserole dish and cook, stirring for 2 minutes until softened. Add the carrot, garlic, tomato purée, flour and chilli powder and stir to combine and cook for a further 2 minutes.

Return the browned meat and all the juices to the casserole dish together with the lemon rind and juice, beef stock and the plum or damson jam. Season well with salt and pepper and bring to a gentle simmer.

Put the lid on the casserole and place in the pre-heated oven for 2 hours until the beef is tender.

Serve with creamed mashed potatoes.

Jane Newton

Lamb Tagine

Although there are lots of ingredients in this recipe it isn't complicated and most of them are used in the marinade. It is a great way to serve lamb and ideal for entertaining.

 Serves 6   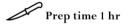 **Prep time 1 hr**   **Marinating time 8 hrs + Cooking time 2 hrs**

Ingredients:

3 tbsp olive oil

1kg diced lamb

2 tsp paprika

¼ tsp ground turmeric

½ tsp ground cumin

¼ tsp cayenne pepper

1 tsp ground cinnamon

¼ tsp ground cloves

½ tsp ground cardamom

1 tsp salt

½ tsp ground ginger

1 pinch saffron

¾ tsp ground coriander

2 medium onions, halved
    and cut into wedges

5 carrots, quartered then
    sliced into thin strips

3 cloves of garlic, crushed

1 tbsp root ginger, grated

1 lemon, zested

400mls chicken stock

1 tbsp tomato purée

1 tbsp honey

1 tbsp cornflour (optional)

100g dried apricots (optional)

Method

Mix the diced lamb with 2 tablespoons of olive oil in a bowl.

Make the marinade by mixing the paprika, turmeric, cumin, cayenne, cinnamon, cloves, cardamom, salt, ginger, saffron, and coriander in a large re-sealable plastic bag. Now add the lamb to the bag and shake it around to make sure the meat is coated with the spice mix. Put in the fridge for at least 8 hours, or ideally overnight.

Heat 1 tablespoon of olive oil in a large, heavy-bottomed casserole dish. Brown the lamb in batches over a high heat. Remove each batch to a plate and put aside. Add the onions and carrots to the casserole and cook for 5 minutes. Add the fresh garlic and root ginger, and cook for another 5 minutes.

Return the lamb to the casserole and add the lemon zest, chicken stock, tomato purée and honey. Bring to the boil, lower the heat, cover and simmer for 1 ½ to 2 hours, stirring occasionally, until the meat is tender. Add the apricots after 1 hour.

If the consistency of the tagine is too thin, thicken it with a mixture of cornflour and water added during the last 5 minutes of cooking.

Serve with couscous and sprinkle with coriander leaves.

Shân Norman

Thai Beef Daube

This gorgeous recipe never fails to please — the combination of a casserole type dish together with an authentic spicy Thai flavour, makes this dish an impressive yet easy entertaining classic and I make no apologies for serving it time and time again!

 Serves 6   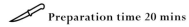 **Preparation time 20 mins**   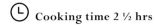 **Cooking time 2 ½ hrs**

Ingredients:

1 tbsp oil

1kg stewing beef, cubed

550g chopped onion

50g grated ginger

1 large red chilli,
   de-seeded and chopped

2 tsp garam masala

4 crushed garlic cloves

400mls can coconut milk

8 lime leaves

4 sticks lemon grass,
   lightly crushed

350g shiitake mushrooms

knob of butter

Method

Pre-heat the oven to 170C.

Heat the oil in a large heavy-based casserole dish and begin to brown the beef in batches over a high heat, then set aside.

Cook the onions until soft (10mins) and then add the ginger, chilli, garam masala and garlic, and cook for a further 5 minutes.

Return the beef to the casserole with the coconut milk, 150mls water, lime leaves and lemon grass. Bring to the boil and season. Cover and cook in the oven for 1½-2 hours or until the beef is tender. The sauce will reduce to a rich gravy, but if it becomes too intense, just add a little boiling water.

Heat the butter in a large frying pan and add the mushrooms, cooking for 5 minutes or until all the juices have evaporated. Stir into the beef.

Serve with Jasmine rice and steamed vegetables.

Maria Lockhart

March Pork Casserole

A tasty casserole dish perfect for a big family gathering, or dinner party with friends.
An old family favourite!

 Serves 6    **Preparation time 30 mins**   **Cooking time 1 ½-2 hrs**

Ingredients:

2 tbsp olive oil

1 green pepper, chopped

1 onion, chopped

2 leeks, washed and sliced

100g button mushrooms,
    washed and cut in half

1-2 tsp curry powder

25g flour

900g diced pork

400g can chopped tomatoes

½ tsp mixed herbs

seasoning

Method

Pre-heat the oven to 160C.

Heat 1 tablespoon of oil in a heavy based frying pan and add the onions, leeks, peppers and mushrooms. Cook for 3-4 minutes and then transfer to a casserole dish.

Add the curry powder and seasoning to the flour and toss the pork in the mixture.

Heat a second tablespoon of oil in the frying pan and brown the pork in small batches, adding to the casserole dish as you do so.

Add the tomatoes and herbs and give the casserole a good stir.

Cover with the lid and cook for 1 ½-2 hours.

Great served with jacket potatoes.

Nadine Pudwell

Lamb Burgers with Beetroot Relish

These burgers have become a real summer staple. Prepare in advance and just stick on the barbecue 10 minutes before you want to eat! Pile the burger into a pitta with sour cream and the beetroot relish for a delicious summer supper.

 Serves 4   Prep time 10 mins   Marinating time 20 mins + Cooking time 10 mins

Ingredients:

Burgers

400g minced lamb

1 garlic clove, crushed

1 tsp ground cumin

*½ bunch of fresh
   coriander, chopped*

1 egg yolk

Beetroot relish

100g cooked beetroot, diced

*1 small red onion,
   finely chopped*

1 bunch of coriander, chopped

1 tbsp red wine vinegar

2 tbsp olive oil

Method

Mix together the ingredients for the relish and leave to stand for at least 20 minutes to allow the flavours to develop.

Put the lamb, garlic, cumin, coriander and egg yolk in a bowl, season well and mix together (hands are best for this). Form into 4 burgers and cook under the grill or on a barbecue for about 5 minutes on each side.

Serve the burgers in warm pitta breads, topped with the beetroot relish.

Juliet Coleman

Mince Beef Pie

Mince Beef Pie

Over the years, this has become a firm family favourite with my children and grandchildren. Not only does it make a great supper dish, but it is ideal as part of a lunchtime buffet at large family gatherings. It is delicious hot or cold and is a great way to use mince.

 Serves 6    **Preparation time 40 mins**   🕐 **Cooking time 1 hr**

Ingredients:

Easy flaky pastry

275g plain flour

225g butter cut into small pieces

chilled water

Filling

1 tbsp cooking oil

500g beef mince

1 onion chopped

1 clove garlic, crushed

2 tbsp tomato purée

2 tbsp Worcestershire sauce

1 tbsp flour

1 tin of tomatoes

100mls red wine

1 beef stock cube

Method

Pre-heat the oven to 180C. Grease a 20cm diameter deep flan dish.

Sift the flour into a large basin, add the butter and cut into the flour until there are small pieces are coated with flour. Add about 6 tablespoons of chilled water, a little at a time, until the pastry comes together. Roll out and fold into three. Repeat this three times, wrap in cling film and put in the fridge to rest for about 30 minutes.

Meanwhile make the filling. Fry the onion in the oil until soft. Add the garlic then the mince and cook until lightly browned. Drain off the fat then add the flour, tomato purée, and Worcestershire sauce. Stir to mix then add a tin of tomatoes. Season with salt and pepper and mix well. Add the beef stock cube and red wine. Leave to simmer for about 30 minutes. Cool.

Put a third of the pastry to one side as this will form the lid of the pie. Roll out the remaining two thirds of the pastry and use to line the base and sides of the flan dish. Bake blind at 200C for about 20 minutes.

Cool slightly then add the cooled filling.

Roll out the remaining pastry and use to cover the pie. Brush with some beaten egg and cook at 180C for about 30 minutes, until pastry is golden.

Hazel Hawkes

Melting Shoulder of Lamb

I begged my mother-in-law for this recipe as slow cooked lamb is fantastic and this really is one of those recipes that you can shove in the oven and forget about. I serve it with mash to soak up the delicious sauce, plenty of green vegetables and lashings of redcurrant jelly or mint sauce. Yum!

 Serves 6    **Preparation time 15 mins**   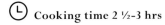 **Cooking time 2 ½-3 hrs**

Ingredients:

1 shoulder of lamb, excess
   fat removed

salt and black pepper

1 tbsp olive oil

30g butter

1 tbsp dried mixed herbs

3 bulbs garlic, separated
   into cloves and peeled

12 shallots peeled and
   left whole

300mls white wine

Method

Pre-heat the oven to 220C.

Place the lamb in a shallow casserole or roasting tin and lightly stab the fat all over. Season the joint and massage in the seasoning.

Brown on the hob with the fat side in the oil and butter, then turn the fat side up and tuck in the garlic and shallots. Pour in the wine and 100mls water, sprinkle with the herbs and bring to the bubble.

Put into a 220C oven un-covered and roast for 30 minutes.

Then turn down the oven to 150C, cover the lamb and slowly braise for 2-2½ hours or until so tender that the meat will fork easily from the bone.

Serve immediately or equally this will re-heat beautifully the next day and taste even more divine.

Lisa Gordon

Mexican Pork Fillets

Great for cold winter months and also for getting rid of any aggression as the more you bash the pork the better! My mum makes this really hot and we all used to fight over the last piece with the best bits of sauce in the bottom of the pot - great with mashed potato to soak up the juices!

 Serves 4    Preparation time 20 mins   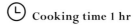 Cooking time 1 hr

Ingredients:

Topping

25g butter

2 cloves garlic, crushed

2-3 chillies, finely chopped

½ tsp ground cumin

1 tsp salt

½ tsp pepper

1 small can tomato purée

Pork

50g flour

700g pork fillets cut into
   steaks and pounded flat

1 tbsp veg oil

400g can peeled tomatoes
   coarsely chopped

½ tsp dried thyme

Method

Pre-heat the oven to 180C.

Mix all the topping ingredients together to form a paste. Spread the mixture onto the pork steaks fairly thickly. Dip them carefully into flour. Heat some oil in a frying pan and brown the steaks mixture side down to start, but be careful as they can stick to pan. Turn and brown the other side.

Place the pork steaks into a casserole and cover with canned tomatoes and thyme. Cook in the oven for about 1 hour or until the pork is tender.

Stella McDonough

Ossobuco

I remember vividly the first time my girlfriend cooked this traditional Italian dish for me… afterwards I asked her to marry me! Happily, she said yes!

 Serves 2    **Preparation time 30 mins**   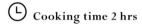 **Cooking time 2 hrs**

Ingredients:

800g (equal to 4 veal shanks, cut into short lengths)

75g flour

1 large onion, finely chopped

2 spring onions, finely chopped

1 small carrot, finely chopped

½ celery stick, finely chopped

240mls dry white wine

3 tbsp olive oil

300g mushrooms

salt and pepper to taste

handful fresh parsley or basil

Method

In a large skillet, heat the olive oil at medium-high temperature. Add the onion, spring onions, carrot and celery. Cook until the onion and the spring onions are gold and tender.

Dust the veal shanks with flour and place them into the skillet together with the vegetables. Cook until browned on both sides, then add white wine, cover and simmer over low heat for 1½ hours, adding the wine when necessary and turn every 15-20 minutes or so.

Wash, dry and coarsely cut the mushrooms and add them to the veal. Season with salt and pepper, cover and simmer over low heat for 15 minutes.

Remove the cover of the skillet and cook at medium-high temperature for an additional 15 minutes. At the end of this stage the water released from mushrooms should have evaporated and the meat should be tender.

Add the parsley or finely cut fresh basil and serve the dish on hot plates.

Paolo Bianchi

Pasta with Lemon, Prosciutto and Chilli

My husband loves this recipe. I always keep the ingredients at home so I can make it when I'm in a hurry.
It's very light and great for a summer lunch or light supper, with a nice glass of chilled white wine!

 Serves 4   **Preparation time 10 mins**   **Cooking time 10 mins**

Ingredients:

60mls lemon juice

60mls extra virgin olive oil

2 small fresh red chillies,
de-seeded and finely
chopped

12 slices prosciutto,
cut into thin strips

1 tbsp grated lemon zest

250g rocket leaves, shredded

400g linguine

grated parmesan to
serve (optional)

Method

Whisk the lemon juice, olive oil, chilli and some salt and pepper in a bowl to blend.

Put the prosciutto, lemon zest and the rocket leaves in a bowl and toss to combine.

Bring a large saucepan of salted water to the boil. Add the linguine and cook until al dente. Drain and add to the prosciutto and rocket. Pour the dressing over and toss with Parmesan to combine.

Transfer to a large serving dish or divide among four bowls.

Kate Fulford

Pork Fillet in a Cream and Mushroom Sauce

This rather retro dish has stood the test of time from London dinner parties in our early twenties to kitchen suppers in our forties! Quick and easy, you can substitute crème fraîche for the double cream if you are feeling healthy!

 Serves 6    Preparation time 10 mins   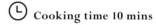 Cooking time 10 mins

Ingredients:

2 medium pork fillets, about
    350g each, cut into strips

50g butter

2 small onions, finely chopped

200g mushrooms, sliced

120mls dry white wine

200mls double cream

2 tbsp chopped fresh
    leaf parsley

salt and pepper

Method

Melt the butter in a large frying pan. Season the meat and cook over a medium heat for 2-3 minutes. Add the onion and cook for 1-2 minutes. Add the mushrooms and cook for 2-3 minutes. Add the white wine, bring the sauce to a boil and boil for a good minute. Stir in the cream. Sprinkle parsley on top to serve.

Helen McAllister

Quick Thai Coconut Beef Stir-Fry

This is one of my favourite dishes at the moment. It is always a success and there is never anything left over.

 Serves 6  Preparation time 15 mins Cooking time 15 mins

Ingredients:

350g rump beef steak

2 tbsp oil

1 bunch of spring onions,
thinly sliced (keep the
white parts and the green
ends separate)

1 red pepper, de-seeded
and thinly sliced

1 tbsp green Thai paste

150g shiitake mushrooms,
halved

225g can of bamboo shoots,
drained (optional)

400mls can of coconut milk

1 tbsp brown sugar

1 lime, grated zest and juice

150g mangetout, thinly sliced

Method

Trim any surplus fat from the steak and beat it out between two pieces of cling film, using a wooden rolling pin, until 1 cm thick. Slice into thin strips.

Heat 1 tablespoon of oil in a frying pan. Brown the beef very quickly in two batches and set aside.

Add the remaining oil and the white parts from the spring onions, the red pepper and the Thai paste to the pan, and stir-fry for a few seconds. Add the mushrooms, bamboo shoots (if using), coconut milk, sugar and lime zest and juice. Bring to the boil and simmer for about 5 minutes.

Add the mangetout and return the beef to the pan, and then simmer for another 3 minutes.

Check the seasoning and adjust if necessary. Sprinkle the green parts from the spring onions over the top.

Turn into warmed bowls and serve with boiled rice.

Gail Williams

Rosti und Geshneltes

This is our family version of the Swiss national dish — we lived there for many years and adopted this as our favourite dish for birthdays and special occasions. The Swiss use veal, but this is expensive, so I use escalopes of pork. My children and grand-children love it and it is easy to make. My vegetarian friend found it easy and acceptable to cook for her family too. Serve with green veg or lambs lettuce side salad.

 Serves 6    **Preparation time 30 mins**   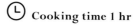 **Cooking time 1 hr**

Ingredients:

Pork

8 - 10 escalopes or medallions of pork (alternatively use veal, turkey or chicken breast)

2 medium white onions

½ chicken or vegetable stock cube in 200mls water

1 tbsp flour

½ large pot crème fraîche

small glass dry sherry (optional, kids prefer without)

Rosti (potato cake)

2kg large potatoes

sunflower/vegetable oil and a knob of butter for the pan

Method

The potatoes should be cooked for about 10 minutes the day before, or earlier on the day of the meal, drained and left somewhere to cool.

To make the rosti, peel and grate the cooled potatoes with the rough side of the grater (I often cheat and use leftover potatoes from the day before to make a small rosti, adjusting the frying time).

Heat the oil and butter in the frying pan and make sure it covers the whole pan including the sides, put the grated potatoes in so it covers the entire pan, about 2 – 3 cm thick, season. Fry on medium to low heat for 10 - 20 min. Use a large flat lid or plate to cover the area of the pan or rosti. Flip over, add some oil to the pan and slip the rosti back in the pan cooking it for another 10-20 min so it is golden brown on both sides.

While the rosti is cooking, cut the meat in small 1 cm wide strips. Coarsely chop the onion and fry until golden brown, set aside.

Fry the meat until it is cooked through, turning as it cooks and set aside somewhere warm.

Put the onion back in the frying-pan, add flour and stock, stirring continuously to make a gravy base. Then add the crème fraîche and the sherry and season to taste. Finally add the warm meat and heat through until it is piping hot and serve with the rosti!

Kristin Rode

Sausage Pasta

This sausage pasta is a great family favourite, made in moments. Children of all ages love it and it can be doubled, trebled or multiplied to feed 5000. It is particularly good for feeding hungry rowers.

 Serves 6 **Preparation time 10 mins** **Cooking time 20 mins**

Ingredients:

2 packs of sausages (I buy
   the chilli ones)

1 large red onion, chopped

2 tins of chopped tomatoes

grated parmesan

450g pasta

Method

Heat some oil in a large pan cook the onion until softened. Skin the sausages, add the meat to the onions, stirring until the sausage-meat has broken up. Add the tomatoes and cook for 20 minutes on a low heat. Stir in grated parmesan to taste.

Serve with pasta.

Emma Armstrong

Scouse

Scousers is the nickname given to the people of Liverpool who are also said to speak with a Scouse accent. It's also the name of a lamb stew. The name Scouse comes from the Norwegian word "lapskaus" which means stew. It was commonly eaten by sailors and it became popular in seaports, like Liverpool, throughout Northern Europe. A vegetarian option without the meat is referred to as Blind Scouse.

Scouse is still a popular meal in Liverpool today and almost every family in Liverpool has their own variation of Scouse but this is mine and best cooked whilst wearing a Liverpool FC shirt!

 Serves 8    **Preparation time 30 mins**   **Cooking time 2-2 ½ hrs**

Ingredients:

2 tbsp oil

500g lamb neck fillets, cubed

500g lamb leg steaks, cubed

2 tbsp plain flour

2 onions, peeled and sliced

500g potatoes, peeled
and sliced

500g swedes or parsnips or
carrots, peeled and cubed

400g tin chopped tomatoes

600mls beef stock

250mls red wine (optional)
or water

1 tbsp thyme, chopped

2 bay leaves

salt and pepper

1 tbsp HP sauce or tomato
ketchup (optional)

Method

Pre-heat oven to 150C.

Dust the lamb in flour. Heat the oil in a casserole dish or a large heavy-based pan and seal the lamb in small batches, placing the browned batches on to a plate.

Now cook the onions for 5 minutes on a moderate heat stirring frequently. Return the browned lamb to the casserole, adding the potatoes, swede/parsnips or carrots and tomatoes. Now stir in the beef stock, wine (if using) and herbs and season well.

Put the lid on the casserole and cook in the oven for 2-2 ½ hours until the lamb is tender, checking at regular intervals and adding more water if required.

Remove from the oven and add the HP sauce or tomato ketchup, stirring well.

This is traditionally served with braised red cabbage and crusty bread.

Mandy Woodard

Slow Roasted Belly Pork, Oyster Sauce and Sweet Potato Confit

I was in my local butcher-shop the other day. Ian, the boss, was enthusing about some grilled belly slices his wife had cooked for dinner, which reminded me of this scrumptious recipe. Belly is quite fatty, so benefits from slow roasting.

Belly of pork doesn't usually feature on the supermarket radar, so you will need to visit a traditional butcher. Ask them to bone and rind the joint for you, a piece of about 2kgs will feed six people. Support your high street butcher, there are only 4860 qualified butchers left in Great Britain, their average age is 55 — with very few apprentices joining the trade.

 Serves 6    **Preparation time 30 mins**   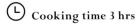 **Cooking time 3 hrs**

Ingredients:

Pork

2kg belly of pork, removed from the bone, rind scored

2 tsp Chinese five-spice powder

Maldon salt, freshly ground pepper

50mls sesame oil

Sweet potato confit

1kg sweet potato, peeled and diced

vegetable oil for cooking

2 garlic cloves, peeled

handful of coriander leaves, chopped

Maldon salt, freshly ground black pepper

1 large red chilli, de-seeded and chopped

Method

Pre-heat oven to 170C.

Put the pork belly in a roasting tray and sprinkle the fat side with Chinese five spice powder salt and pepper. Pour a little sesame oil over and bake in the pre-heated oven for 3 hours. When crispy skinned, tender succulent meat, remove from oven, rest for 15 minutes, slice before serving.

Meanwhile make the sweet potato confit. Put the sweet potatoes in a pan and cover with oil. Add the garlic and cook slowly until the potatoes are tender. Drain off the oil before serving. Sprinkle over the coriander, chilli and seasoning. I accompany my pork and potato with wok sautéed Bok Choi and a drizzle of hoi sin.

Paul Clerehugh – Chef

Spaghetti Carbonara

This is a quick and easy supper dish which is always popular.

 Serves 4    **Preparation time 20 mins**

Ingredients:

1 small pot thick double cream

2 egg yolks

grated parmesan

cubed pancetta (available
  smoked or non smoked in
  cute little pots from
  supermarkets or any bacon
  or pancetta will do)

150g spaghetti

salt and pepper

spinach to garnish

Method

Cook the pasta according to instructions.

While the pasta is cooking, prepare the sauce. Fry the cubed pancetta until crispy, drain and keep to one side. Separate the yolks from the eggs, discarding the whites. Put the yolks in a bowl and add in half the pot of double cream and mix. Adjust the amount of cream according to taste and how runny you like the sauce. Add the grated parmesan until the sauce has a thick consistency (you can always add more egg yolks / double cream / parmesan until right consistency is achieved. I like it when it resembles thick custard)

Drain the cooked pasta and add the carbonara sauce. The residual heat of the pasta and saucepan is enough to cook the egg yolks (but don't overcook or it turns to scrambled eggs!) Add in the crispy pancetta and stir.

Serve with spinach on the side, adding salt and pepper to taste.

For hungry mouths, add garlic bread.

Sarah Tuckwell

Vegetarian

Indian Potato Cakes with Mint Chutney

These traditional potato cakes are known as Aloo Tikki. The recipe is one my mother used to make and I now make for my children. They make a great starter served with mint chutney.

 Serves 4    Preparation time 30 mins

Ingredients:

Potato Cakes

450g potatoes, peeled and
    chopped into 1cm cubes

2 red chillies, deseeded
    and finely chopped

1 bunch spring onions,
    roughly chopped

salt and pepper

olive oil

Mint chutney

2 tbsp mint sauce

1 large onion, peeled
    and sliced

2 green chillies

½ tsp salt

1 tsp cumin seeds

1 tsp sugar

Method

To make the potato cakes, cook the potatoes in boiling water or in a covered dish in the microwave, until soft. Add all the remaining ingredients and mash together roughly. Shape dessert spoonfuls of the mixture into flat cakes.

Brush the tops of the cakes with a little oil and cook them in a large heavy based frying pan oiled side down for about 2 minutes until golden brown. Brush the tops of the cakes with a little more oil, turn them over and cook for a further 1-2 minutes. Drain them on kitchen paper and keep them warm while cooking the remainder.

To make the mint chutney, dry roast the cumin seeds in a heavy based frying pan. Place all the ingredients in a blender and mix together.

The mint chutney can be made the day before and stored in the fridge.

Salinder Hunjan

Sweet Chilli Butterbeans

I love pulses and this is a fantastic way of cooking butterbeans, as they soak up all the flavours. It makes a great alternative to Mediterranean recipes.

 Serves 6   **Prep time 25 mins**   **Soaking time 12 hrs + Cooking time 35-55 mins**

Ingredients:

400g dried butterbeans

6 garlic cloves, crushed

70mls sweet chilli sauce

2 tbsp sesame oil

3 tbsp soy sauce

3 tbsp lemon juice

2 red peppers, deseeded and cut into 2 cm squares

4 spring onions, chopped

35g coriander, chopped

30g mint leaves, chopped

salt and black pepper

Method

Put the butterbeans in a large bowl, add water to double the volume of the beans and leave to soak overnight at room temperature.

Drain the beans and place in a large saucepan. Cover with cold water and bring to the boil. Simmer for 35-55 minutes, until tender. Check the beans regularly, top up the water and remove the froth from the surface. Cooking time will depend on the bean size and freshness, so check them regularly to make sure they don't turn to a mush. If they start to overcook, cool them quickly by adding cold water. Drain in a colander and leave to one side.

While the beans are cooking, make the sauce. Place the crushed garlic in a large bowl. Add the sweet chilli sauce, sesame oil, soy sauce and lemon juice and whisk together. Add the red peppers, season the mixture with salt and pepper and set aside.

Once the beans have cooled a little but are still warm, add them to the sauce, together with the spring onions, herbs and plenty of seasoning. Mix gently with your hands. Taste and adjust the seasoning.

Eat warm or cold.

Maria Fernandez de Pinedo

Chickpeas with Spinach and Spices

Looking for something to conjure up the essence of the Middle East, something warm and spicy and full of flavour? Well, here it is, suitable as a main course or as a side dish, it is best supplemented with a light rice dish. Try giving the rice some flavour by adding a bit of spice using coriander, almonds and a few raisins. The Casbah will suddenly seem a lot nearer.

 Serves 4    **Preparation time 25 mins**   **Cooking time 10-15 mins**

Ingredients:

2 tbsp water

1 medium onion, chopped

3 cloves garlic, crushed

1 tsp ground cinnamon

1 tsp ground sweet paprika

2 tbsp ground coriander

2 tbsp cumin seeds

3 x 425g cans chick peas
 rinsed and drained

3 medium tomatoes chopped

2 tbsp tomato paste

40g seeded chopped dates

250mls water, extra

2 tbsp chopped fresh coriander
 leaves

2 tbsp chopped mint

500g spinach chopped

Method

Combine the water, onion, garlic and spices in a large pan and cook, stirring until soft.

Stir in the chickpeas, tomatoes, paste and dates. Add the extra water and herbs. Simmer covered for 10 minutes.

Stir in spinach, simmer uncovered for about 5 minutes or until spinach is just wilted.

Sally Oxley

110

Grilled Halloumi with Corn Salad

This is such a light, refreshing salad, and we just love the salty, somewhat rubbery Halloumi.

 Serves 2    Preparation time 15 mins   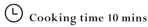 Cooking time 10 mins

Ingredients:

Salad

1 pack halloumi cheese

1 tbsp olive oil

1 small tin sweetcorn

4 or 5 spring onions, chopped

1 small red chilli, finely sliced

1 tsp coriander, chopped

Dressing

juice of 1 lemon

salt and pepper

2 tbsp olive oil

Method

To make the dressing combine the oil, lemon juice and seasoning.

Put the drained corn, spring onions, chilli and chopped coriander in a bowl and toss with the dressing.

Slice the halloumi into 8 pieces and brush with a little olive oil.

Heat a skillet or a griddle pan and lightly brown the halloumi on both sides, for about 3 minutes.

Place some corn salad on a serving plate and arrange the halloumi on top. Drizzle with a little olive oil.

Roz Kempner

Grilled Halloumi with Corn Salad

Mango Vegetable Salad

I first ate this salad at a friend's house on a humid Boxing Day in Singapore. She is a great cook and whenever I make it always reminds me of her. It looks and tastes great.

 Serves 6-8   Preparation time 20 mins

Ingredients:

Salad

2 medium mangoes

2 medium carrots

2 medium courgettes

1 medium red pepper

1 medium yellow pepper

1 ½ cups of bean sprouts

2 spring onions

¼ cup fresh coriander, chopped

1 cup salted nuts

Dressing

⅓ cup olive oil

¼ cup freshly squeezed orange juice

2 tbsp white vinegar

1 tsp cracked black pepper

1 tbsp peanut butter

1 clove garlic, finely chopped or crushed

Method

Peel and cut the mango flesh into strips. Peel the carrots then cut the carrots and courgettes into thin strips lengthways with a vegetable peeler. Slice the red and yellow peppers and spring onions into thin strips.

Whisk all the dressing ingredients together in a small bowl.

Combine all the salad ingredients together in a large bowl and drizzle over the dressing.

Stir to combine.

Nicola Williams

Gnocchi with Mushroom Ragu

 Serves 4

Ingredients:

600g floury potato, like russet

450g flour

1 large egg, beaten

salt and pepper

1 onion, finely chopped

1 carrot, finely chopped

1 stick celery, finely chopped

4 cloves garlic

150g tomato paste

450mls red wine

450mls stock

fresh rosemary

shaved pecorino to serve

mushrooms eg field, shitake

Method

To make the gnocchi, boil the potatoes for about 25 minutes until soft, drain, but don't add any water to cool them.

When cool enough to handle pass through a ricer or mash. Make a well in the centre, add the egg and seasoning. Now add the flour and mix to form a dough. Knead for a few minutes. Divide the mixture into 4 or 5 pieces and roll out into 20mm diameter ropes, then cut off at 25mm intervals.

Drop the small pieces into boiling water and when they rise to the top, scoop them out and refresh in ice-water. Drain, oil and keep warm.

To make the ragu, gently fry the onion, carrot and celery for 5 minutes until soft. Add the tomato paste and cook for 7-8 minutes until rich red. This really releases so much flavour. Add the wine, stock and rosemary, bring to boil, and simmer for about 45 mins to I hour.

Add the gnocchi to the sauce and allow to thicken.

Serve with the cooked mushrooms (cooked in butter) and cheese.

Simon Rimmer - Chef

Noodle Salad

All children love this salad and it is very easy to make for a large number as part of a buffet.

 Serves 4-6    **Preparation time 20 mins**

Ingredients:

Salad

1 x 250g pack of medium egg
    noodles

6 baby carrots, sliced

75g sugarsnap peas

6 spring onions, finely sliced

5g coriander leaves, chopped

salt

Dressing

3 tbsp red or white vinegar

2 tbsp soy sauce

2 tbsp sesame oil

4 tbsp groundnut oil

1 tbsp caster sugar

1 clove garlic, finely chopped

¼ tsp ground coriander

2.5cm piece of root ginger,
    peeled and grated

10g fresh coriander

pepper

Method

Place all dressing ingredients into a blender and whisk together.

Meanwhile cook the noodles according to the packet. Drain and douse under cold running water to stop the cooking process. Drain and put in a larger serving bowl. Dress immediately.

Bring a pan of water to the boil and blanch the carrots and peas. Cool under running water and add to the noodle salad with the spring onions. Toss again and sprinkle with coriander leaves.

Kate Sloane

Potatoes O'Brien

When I left from home in the early 80's I started collecting cookery magazines and this was one of the recipes I discovered. I tried it for a dinner party and had so many compliments that I have been using it ever since. It goes with absolutely everything and have even served it with Chicken Jalfrezi!! As my mum is not keen on cheese, when I made it for her I substituted the gruyere for cheddar and it worked just as well.

 Serves 6    **Preparation time 15 mins**   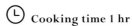 **Cooking time 1 hr**

Ingredients:

1kg floury potatoes

1 large green pepper, seeded and finely chopped

1 large Spanish onion, finely chopped

1 tbsp flour

4 tbsp finely chopped parsley

100g Gruyère cheese, grated

pinch of cayenne pepper

salt and freshly ground black pepper

25g butter

150mls hot milk

150mls thick cream

Method

Pre-heat the oven to 200C.

Peel the potatoes and cut into 1 cm dice and place in a large bowl. Add the chopped green pepper and onion to the potatoes and toss lightly with a large fork to mix. Sprinkle in the flour, finely chopped parsley and grated Gruyère cheese and toss again. Season carefully with a pinch of cayenne pepper, salt and a little freshly ground black pepper.

Use some of the butter to grease a 1.7L ovenproof dish.

Turn the potato mixture into the dish and spread it evenly. Pour over the hot milk and the cream and dot the remaining butter over the top.

Bake in the oven for about 1 hour, until the surface is crisp and golden brown and the potatoes feel tender when pierced with a skewer.

Serve immediately.

Sally Cowens

Quinoa and Beetroot with Balsamic Vinegar

Two very 'worthy' ingredients that don't really make you go 'mm', but I promise you will like this!
Plus, it is ever so quick and makes a great side dish for grilled chicken, roasted fish, or even tofu.
Children will love the colour.

 Serves 2-4   **Preparation time 30 mins**

Ingredients:

100g quinoa, well washed
under cold water (use a fine
mesh sieve)

250g water

1 small beetroot, scrubbed and
peeled

3 tbsp pumpkin seeds or pine
nuts, lightly pan-toasted

2 cardamom pods, seeds only
– ground (optional)

10g parsley, chopped

1 tbsp thick balsamic vinegar

a few grinds of black pepper

Method

Put the rinsed quinoa into a saucepan with the cold water. Bring to the boil, cover and reduce the heat; simmer for 6 minutes. Turn off the heat and allow the quinoa to steam with the lid on for about five minutes. The water should have absorbed after this time and the tiny seeds will have sprouted a tail (!)

Finely grate the beetroot into the quinoa, then add the remaining ingredients. Give it all a good stir and serve.

Note: In addition to the pepper I usually add five ground coriander seeds and the ground seeds of 2 cardamom pods, but don't get these ingredients especially, it's just as tasty without.

Kellie Anderson – Nutrition Advisor
Maggie's Cancer Caring Centres

Portobello Mushrooms in Puff Pastry with Red Onion and Tomato Sauce

A steamy little number, that warms the cockles of the heart. Breaking the puff pastry allows all those sumptuous flavours to be released. A favourite with those that want a tasty vegetarian dish. Even meat eaters have been tempted.

 Serves 4    Preparation time 30 mins   Cooking time 25 mins

Ingredients:

1 x 225g block puff pastry
defrosted (or use ready
rolled puff pastry)

4 portobello mushrooms
(preferably organic ones as
they taste better)

4 tsp Worcestershire sauce
(optional)

1 large red onion, chopped

1 clove garlic, finely chopped

1 tin of tomatoes

2 tsp balsamic vinegar

½ tsp salt and black pepper

1 tsp sugar

milk for glazing

Method

Pre-heat the oven to 220C.

Heat some oil in a frying pan and gently cook the onions and garlic for 10 minutes or until soft. Add tomatoes, Worcestershire sauce, vinegar, salt, pepper and sugar and simmer for 15 minutes.

Divide the pastry into quarters, roll out into squares approx 20 cm long and leave to stand for a few minutes.

Brush the gills of the mushrooms with the Worcestershire sauce if using. Spoon the tomato mixture into the mushrooms, being careful not to over fill them. Place them on a square of pastry, fold the pastry over the mushrooms so that the corners overlap at the top and press the edges together as firmly as possible.

Lightly brush with milk, cut a couple of steam slits in the top of the pastry and bake for 25 minutes.

Sally Oxley

Tricolore Couscous Salad

This yummy salad is always a winner. It is quick and easy to put together and makes a lovely supper.

 Serves 4  **Preparation time 15 mins**

Ingredients:

Salad

200g couscous

2 tsp vegetable stock powder

250g cherry tomatoes, halved

2 avocados, peeled, stoned and chopped

150g mozzarella, drained and chopped

handful rocket or young spinach leaves

Dressing

1 tbsp pesto

1 tbsp lemon juice

3 tbsp olive oil

Method

Mix the couscous and stock powder in a bowl, pour over 300mls boiling water then cover with a plate and leave for 5 minutes.

For the dressing, mix the pesto with the lemon juice and some seasoning. Gradually mix in the oil. Pour over the couscous and mix with a fork.

Mix the tomatoes, avocado and mozzarella into the couscous.

Lightly stir in the rocket or spinach to serve.

Lisa Burrows

Rotolo Di Pasta with Mushroom, Marscapone and Walnut Filling

 Serves 6

Ingredients:

500g cleaned and chopped wild fresh mushrooms

50g dried porcini mushrooms, soaked in warm water for 3 minutes, then drained and chopped, reserve liquid

2 tbsp unsalted butter

300g fresh mascarpone

60g finely chopped walnuts

150g freshly grated Parmigiano

2 eggs, beaten

2 tbsp freshly chopped flat leaf parsley

sea salt

freshly ground black pepper

Method

Gently sauté the fresh and dried mushrooms together with the butter, stirring frequently. Strain the reserved liquid and use this to baste the cooking mushrooms if necessary. When they are soft, dry and thoroughly cooked, set aside to cool completely. Chop or process finely, then stir in the mascarpone, chopped walnuts, the Parmigiano, beaten eggs, chopped parsley and seasoning. Set aside until required.

Make the pasta as normal using 5 eggs, 250 g semola or finest semolina and 250g plain white flour and roll into a wide sheet with a rolling pin. The size of the sheet will depend on how large your cloth is, you will need to allow enough fabric at each end of the roll to be able to tie the cloth securely in place, and also how long or wide your fish kettle/pan is going to be. Spread the filling evenly and not too thickly over the sheet and then roll the pasta up like a "Swiss Roll" making sure there is no air between each turn of the spiral. Keep within 3 centimetres of the edges of the cloth. Wrap it tightly in a clean muslin cloth or large napkin. Tie the ends tightly. Bring a fish kettle or wide pan of salted water to the boil. Slide the wrapped roll into the water carefully and boil gently for about 45 minutes. DON'T LET IT SAG IN THE CENTRE. Remove carefully and drain. Unwrap and lay on a board to slice with a very sharp knife. Arrange the slices on a plate and spoon over a little tomato sauce or melted butter. Any leftover filling can be used to simply toss through freshly cooked pasta as a simple, rich and effective sauce.

N.B. One thing that is really useful about this dish is that it can sit quite happily in the hot water, once cooked, until you are ready to serve it, for up to about 30 minutes. Another point worth mentioning is that you should make sure the cloth is not saturated in fabric conditioner as this will really affect the flavour of the dish.

Valentina Harris – Chef

Shitake and Sesame Noodles

Delicious and super quick, meat free and quite healthy

 **Serves 4**   **Preparation time 30 mins**

Ingredients:

250g medium egg noodles

2 tbsp olive oil

300g shiitake mushrooms

2 bunches spring onions

1 packet fine green beans

2 tbsp sesame seeds

2 tbsp sesame oil

2 tbsp soy sauce

2 tbsp mirin (Japanese sweet
   cooking wine)

Method

Boil the noodles according to the packet instructions. Drain and return to the pan with a little cooking water and sesame oil.

Slice the shiitake mushrooms.

Trim the spring onions and cut into 3cm lengths.

Dry roast the sesame seeds until golden. Tip onto a plate.

Cut the beans into thirds.

Add the olive oil and shiitake mushrooms to a wok and stir-fry for a few minutes until beginning to wilt. Add the spring onions and beans and continue to fry for 5 minutes. Add the soy sauce and mirin and a dash more of sesame oil, letting them bubble up. Add a dash of water if it gets too dry.

Return the noodles and heat through together. Serve with the sesame seeds scattered over.

Fiona Mates

Sin Free Squash and Pepper Stacks

Delicious and super quick, meat free and quite healthy

 Serves 10

Ingredients:

430g rice

375g red onions

250g feta cheese

25g parsley

2½ large red peppers

6 tbsp olive oil

1 tsp all spice

1 tsp cardamom seeds

50g raisins

3 butternut squash

25mls balsamic vinegar

salt and pepper

250g cranberry sauce

1½ tsp lemon juice

Method

Place a pan of water onto the stove and bring to the boil, add the rice and cook for approximately 10 minutes or until the rice is tender. Drain well and season. Keep hot.

Peel and chop the onions very finely, dice the feta, chop the parsley and cut the peppers into 10 thick slices.

Heat a saucepan and add 1 tablespoon of olive oil. Cook the onions until soft and lightly coloured. Add the spice and cardamom seeds, followed by the raisins and cook for 2 minutes. Add to the rice along with the diced feta and chopped parsley, keep hot.

Peel the squash and cut into 20 circles, approx 1 cm thick. Blanch in boiling salted water for 2-3 minutes to slightly soften, then refresh in cold water and dry.

Mix the remaining olive oil with the balsamic vinegar and brush the squash and peppers.

Heat a griddle pan and char-grill the squash and peppers making sure to mark evenly. Keep hot until you are ready to assemble.

Melt the cranberry sauce, add a little water until the required consistency is reached. Add the lemon juice.

To assemble the stacks, place a spoonful of the rice mixture onto one of the squash circles and top with a second piece of squash. Spoon over a little of the cranberry sauce and garnish with a slice of grilled pepper.

Helen Potter - Chef at Rugby School

Tuk Tuk Salad

This has become a stalwart for large gatherings. It's like the porridge pot, no matter how much you eat, the bowl never seems to empty. It brings back memories of happy, sunny afternoons in my big sister's garden, surrounded by kids and dogs and empty wine bottles. Leftovers last for a good few days and are delicious with cold meat or grilled fish.

 Serves 6    **Preparation time 30 mins**

Ingredients:

Salad

150g brown basmati rice

100g wild rice (it is a pain to find, but worth it — avoid the mixed bags)

125g frozen peas

100g frozen soya beans (or broad beans if you have the time to double pod)

2 bunches salad onions, finely chopped

2 plum tomatoes, roughly chopped

50g rocket leaves

2 tbsp toasted seeds (mixed sunflower, linseed etc)

2 tbsp chopped coriander

Dressing

1 red chilli, very finely chopped

3 cm fresh root ginger, grated

1 small garlic clove, very finely chopped

1 lime, juiced and extra limes, quartered to serve

3 tbsp sesame oil

3 tbsp soy sauce

Method

Cook each kind of rice separately, according to instructions on the packet.

Meanwhile, whisk the ingredients for the dressing together and leave to infuse.

Drain each batch of rice into a sieve and run under cool water. Mix them together in a bowl.

Blanch the peas and soya beans. Rinse with cold water then stir into the rice with the salad onions and some salt. Mix in the dressing until everything is well coated.

In a small bowl, mix together the tomatoes, rocket, seeds and coriander and spoon them over the top of the rice. Serve with quarters of lime.

Tessa Murray

Ian's Warm Potato Salad

Simplicity itself, a perfect companion for summer barbecues, salmon and picnics, this made its al fresco debut at The Henley Festival in 2004 and now appears regularly on the terraces of Oxfordshire and Cornwall. One for the man in the house to prepare.

 Serves 6-8   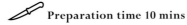 **Preparation time 10 mins**   **Cooking time 25 mins**

Ingredients:

1kg new potatoes (Jersey
    Royals the best but any
    good new ones will do)

8 to 10 spring onions

5 sprigs of mint

150g butter

1 to 2 tbsp Hellman's
    mayonnaise

salt and freshly milled black
    pepper

Method

Gently scrub, wash and then chop the potatoes into bite size halves or quarters and ideally steam until cooked.

Whilst they are steaming prepare the spring onions. Top and tail them but be sure to leave a good amount of the green top shoots which as well as being tasty provide a lovely sharp green colour to the dish, then chop the onions roughly into half centimetre pieces.

Once the potatoes are cooked, they should be firm not squidgy, remove the saucepan from the direct heat, add the mint sprigs to the potatoes and replace the pan lid. Leave for 5 minutes for the mint to infuse into the new potatoes.

Remove the mint and transfer the potatoes to a warm serving dish and add the chopped onions and butter. Gently fold the butter into the mix until melted, add salt to taste if required, and lots of freshly milled black pepper. Finally add the Hellman's and fold into the potatoes so that they are lightly coated with the mayonnaise.

Serve warm initially but can be reheated the following day.

Ian Whittaker

Hot puddings

Cow Pat Pudding

This pudding can be made from ingredients in the store cupboard and is always a firm favourite. Doubled or trebled it works!

 Serves 6    **Preparation time 15 mins**   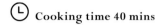 **Cooking time 40 mins**

Ingredients:

Pudding

90g self-raising flour

120g butter

120g caster sugar

1-2 tbsp milk

2 level tbsp cocoa

2 eggs

Sauce

120g soft brown sugar

2 tbsp cocoa

300mls water

Method

Pre-heat the oven to 190C.

Sift the flour and cocoa powder and mix together in a bowl.

Cream the butter and sugar until pale and fluffy. Beat in the eggs one at a time followed by the milk. Gently fold in the flour and cocoa. Put the mixture into a buttered ovenproof dish.

To make the sauce, put the sugar and cocoa and water in a saucepan and bring to the boil. Pour this over the uncooked cake mixture and bake in the oven for 40 minutes.

Leave for 10 minutes and serve. The pudding develops its own sauce.

Jane Kibble

Chocolate and Raspberry Pudding

This is a delicious pudding and sooo... simple to make! Your guests and family will be delighted with your choice.

 Serves 4    Preparation time 15 mins   Cooking time 15 mins

Ingredients:

45g butter plus extra for
   greasing

120g frozen raspberries (or
   any red berries)

150g plain chocolate – broken
   into small pieces

75g caster sugar

2 eggs separated

½ tsp vanilla essence

2 tbsp icing sugar

Method

Pre-heat the oven to 200C.

Butter the sides of 4 x 175mls ramekins, divide the berries between them.

Melt the chocolate with the butter in a bowl over a pan of simmering water.

Whisk the sugar and egg yolks with an electric whisk until light and creamy, then stir in the vanilla.

In another bowl whisk the egg whites into soft peaks.

Fold the chocolate and butter mixture into the whisked egg yolks. Then fold in the egg whites with a large metal spoon.

Spoon the mixture into the ramekins and bake on a baking sheet for 12-14 minutes until risen but slightly wobbly. Dust with icing sugar to serve.

Jill Hatton

Pear and Chocolate Frangipane Tart

Pears and chocolate first came to my attention at school. Canned pears, that is, with lumpy chocolate custard.
It was my favourite pudding and I'd try to blend back into the dinner queue to lots of jostling elbows and shouts
of 'Warner sod off, you've already had some!' If you like this recipe, by all means have some more.

 Serves 8    **Prep time 35-40 mins**   **Cooking time 1 hr + Chilling time 1 hr**

Ingredients:

Pastry

250g plain flour, plus extra
　for dusting

150g fridge-cold unsalted
　butter, cut into small pieces

2 tbsp caster sugar

1 medium free-range egg,
　beaten

Filling

150g plain chocolate

175g unsalted butter, softened

175g caster sugar

125g ground almonds

75g plain flour

½ tsp flaked sea salt

½ tsp baking powder

2 medium free-range eggs,
　beaten

¼ tsp vanilla extract

3 ripe (but not squishy)
　conference pears

juice of ½ lemon

15g flaked almonds

crème fraîche or cream,
　to serve

Method

Pre-heat the oven 200C.

To make the pastry, put the flour, butter and sugar in a food processor and blend until the mixture resembles fine breadcrumbs. With the motor running, slowly add the egg to the flour mixture. Turn off the motor as soon as the dough forms a ball. Wrap the pastry in cling film and pop it in the fridge for an hour or so.

Roll out the pastry on a well-floured surface to the thickness of a £1 coin, lifting and turning after every few rolls, then use it to line a deep, fluted 25cm tart case. Don't worry if the pastry tears a little, simply repair any gaps with the trimmings. Really tuck the pastry down into the corners and leave it to overhang the sides of the tart case until cooked, and then trim it. This will prevent the pastry from shrinking below the rim, as it so often does when pre-trimmed. Place on a sturdy baking tray and prick the base lightly with a fork. Line the pastry case with crumpled baking parchment and fill with baking beans. Bake blind for 22 minutes then remove the paper and beans and cook for a further minutes, or until the base is dry.

Remove from the oven and put to one side while the filling is prepared. Reduce the oven temperature to 170°C

Slam the chocolate, in its wrapper, on to the table to break it up into big chunks or, if feeling more peaceful, cut instead. Personally I prefer a little drama.

In a food processor, blend the butter and sugar until pale and soft. Add the almonds, flour, salt, baking powder, eggs and vanilla extract. Blend well. Remove the blade and stir in the chocolate pieces with a spatula. Spread the almond mixture evenly over the cooled pastry case, starting around the edge before heading into the centre.

Peel the pears and cut into quarters. Remove the cores and put all the pear quarters into a large bowl and dress with a little squeeze of lemon juice. Arrange the pear quarters pregnant side upwards and with the narrow ends towards the middle, pressing them gently into the almond batter.

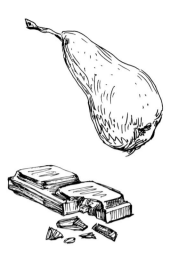

Method - Continued...

Bake the tart on a tray in the centre of the oven for 30 minutes. Remove from the oven, sprinkle all over with flaked almonds, then return to the oven for a further 35–40 minutes, or until the pears are tender and the frangipane filling is well risen and golden brown.

Leave to stand for 15 minutes before lifting from the tin. Ideally, time this so the tart is served warm. Mind you, it's good cold, too, or at room temperature. It is an offence to serve this without crème fraîche or cream.

Valentine Warner _ Chef

Apple Crunch

This is a recipe my sister Felicity brought back from Canada, where she lived for a couple of years about 30 years ago. We've both used it hundreds of times over the years, especially for Sunday lunch, and although it's very simple and incredibly easy to throw together, for some reason people always rave about it. I think the secret is to press it down well on top of the apples to form more of a crust than a crumble and that's what gives it a "crunch".

 Serves 6  Preparation time 20 mins Cooking time 30 mins

Ingredients:

6-8 apples, peeled, cored and sliced

175g demerara sugar

50g plain flour

50g oats

75g butter

¼ tsp cinnamon

¾ tsp nutmeg

Method

Pre-heat the oven to 190C.

Place all ingredients apart from the apples in a food processor and blend until the butter starts to bring the mixture slightly together but still crumbly.

Put the sliced apples into an ovenproof dish and drizzle over about ¼ cup of water. Sprinkle the crumble mixture on top and spread so that all the apples are covered. Press down so that the topping is flat and packed down all over.

Bake in the oven for about ½ hour, or until the topping is golden and crunchy.

Serve with vanilla ice cream, custard or crème fraîche

Charlotte Tompkins

Dutch Apple Pie

This is a great alternative to the traditional English apple pie and is a dessert that I always make at Christmas. You can use ready made pastry but the sweet pastry is worth making and has a lovely lemon flavour.

 Serves 8    **Preparation time 40 mins**   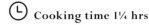 **Cooking time 1¼ hrs**

Ingredients:

Pastry

350g plain flour

175g butter cut into small pieces

225g caster sugar

1 egg, beaten

grated rind of a lemon

Filling

900g cooking apples

110g sultanas

50g caster sugar

1 tsp cinnamon

Method

Pre-heat the oven to 180C. Grease a 20cm diameter loose bottom tin.

Sift the flour add the butter and rub into the flour with your finger tips until the texture is like fine breadcrumbs. Alternatively place flour and butter pieces in a food processor and blend until the texture is like fine breadcrumbs. Add the sugar and lemon rind and mix gently. Add the beaten egg and mix until the pastry starts to come together, then use your hand to knead together.

Cut about 1/6 pastry to use for the trellis topping and roll out the rest. Line the base and sides of the tin with the pastry, pressing the pastry firmly into the sides. Don't worry if the pastry cracks or breaks, just patch it up with more pastry and press together firmly. Add the pastry trimmings to the pastry set aside for the trellis topping.

Peel and slice apples. Mix sugar and cinnamon together. Place a layer of apples on the pastry base and sprinkle with the sugar and cinnamon mixture. Continue layering apples and sugar until the apples are used up.

Roll out the remaining pastry and cut in to 10 long strips about 2.5 cm wide. Lay five strips horizontally across the top of the pie leaving even spaces between each strip. Press one end of each strip onto the pastry sides to seal. Lay the other five strips of pastry vertically and weave each one under and over the horizontal strips to form a trellis. Press the ends of each pastry strip onto the pastry forming the side of the pie to seal.

Sprinkle the top of the pie with sugar and bake in the oven for 1 to 1¼ hours.

Serve hot or cold.

Hazel Hawkes

Cider Baked Apples with Maize Crust

Serve this mulled pie with thick Dorset cream or vanilla ice-cream

 Serves 6-8   Cooking time 40-45 mins

Ingredients:

Pastry

140g plain flour

55g instant dried polenta or semolina

pinch salt

115g butter

1 large egg, beaten

cold water

Filling

6 large dessert apples, peeled, cored and halved

55g unsalted butter, melted

150mls fruity cider

25g soft brown sugar

sprig rosemary

caster sugar for sprinkling

Method

Pre-heat the oven to 200C.

Into a large bowl, sieve the flour, salt and polenta. Rub in the butter until the mixture resembles fine breadcrumbs. Stir in the egg and enough water to bind the dough together. Chill the pastry for 30 minutes.

Place the apples in a shallow, round ovenproof dish approx. 23cm in diameter. Combine the melted butter with the cider and pour over the apples. Sprinkle the apples with the brown sugar and tuck in the sprig of rosemary.

On a lightly floured surface, roll out the pastry until it is large enough to lay as a blanket over the apples. Carefully lift the pastry over the apples and roughly trim the edges and tuck inside the dish. Lightly sprinkle the pastry with the caster sugar.

Bake the pie for 10 minutes, then reduce the oven to 170C. Bake for a further 30-35 minutes until the apples are softened and cooked.

Lesley Waters - Chef

Dutch Apple Pie

Sticky Pear Pudding with Caramel Sauce

If you have a huge crop of pears (or apples) in the autumn this is a fab alternative to crumble or pie, and the kids love it!! Delicious served with cream or ice cream.

 Serves 6    Preparation time 15 mins   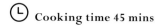 Cooking time 45 mins

Ingredients:

4 large ripe pears, peeled, cored and sliced

125g plain flour

2 tsp baking powder

125g caster sugar

200mls milk

75g butter melted

1 medium egg, beaten

150g light brown muscovado sugar

4 tbsp golden syrup

Method

Pre-heat the oven to 180C.

Arrange the pear slices in the base of a buttered 1.5 litre ovenproof dish.

Sift the flour and baking powder together into a bowl and add the caster sugar, milk, melted butter and egg. Whisk together for 2-3 minutes until pale in colour, then pour over the pears.

To make the caramel sauce, place the muscovado sugar and syrup in a small pan and add 250mls cold water. Cook over a moderate heat, stirring until the sugar has dissolved. With no further stirring allow to reach boiling point, then remove from the heat.

Carefully pour the sauce over the pudding then bake for 35-40 minutes before serving with cream or vanilla ice cream.

The pears can be replaced with 4 dessert apples, peeled, cored and sliced and you can also add 1 tsp ground cinnamon to the sponge mix.

Liz Sim

Spicy Plums with Brûlée Cream

A few of our husbands got together to see who was the best cook. After five extremely competitive dinner parties, the winner of "Come Dine with Him" was crowned! This top scoring pudding was the reason he won it!

 Serves 8-10   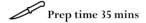 **Prep time 35 mins**   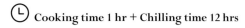 **Cooking time 1 hr + Chilling time 12 hrs**

Ingredients:

Spicy plums

2.kg plums

1 bottle of red wine

4 bay leaves

2 cinnamon sticks or a tsp
   ground cinnamon

4 cloves

2 star anise

½ ground cardamom

750g honey (either runny or
   thick)

Brûlée cream

750mls double cream

750mls Greek yogurt

150g light muscovado sugar or
   more as needed.

Method

Pre-heat the oven to 170C.

Make the brûlée cream a day in advance. Mix the cream and Greek yogurt together then beat till fairly thick. Pour into a shallow bowl and sprinkle the surface with a good coating of brown sugar. Cover with cling film and put in the fridge for at least 12 hours, or better still 24.

To prepare the plums, cut them in half, remove the stones and divide them between 2 shallow baking dishes, cut side down.

Put all the other ingredients into a saucepan and bring to the boil. Pour over the plums, cover the baking dishes tightly with foil (or a lid, of course, if you have one that fits) and bake in the pre-heated oven for 1 hr, or until the plums are tender.

Serve warm with Brûlée Cream

Beverley Rodick

Spicy Plums with Brûlée Cream

Hot Plum Torte

This is an easy and delicious pudding that can be made in advance and kept in the fridge before cooking. It also works well with apples and pears.

 Serves 8  **Preparation time 30 mins** 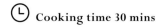 **Cooking time 30 mins**

Ingredients:

75g soft butter

75g caster sugar

100g self-raising flour

1 tsp baking powder

2 large eggs

finely grated zest of 1 orange

900g ripe plums, cut in half, stones removed

150g demerara sugar

Method

Pre-heat the oven to 200C.

Butter a 28cm by 4cm ovenproof dish or deep loose bottomed flan tin.

Put the butter, sugar, flour, baking powder, eggs and orange zest into a large bowl and beat until smooth. Spread this mixture evenly over the bottom of the tin or dish.

Arrange the plums on top, cut side up and sprinkle with the demerara sugar to form a thick layer. (The torte can be made completely to this point and kept uncooked in the fridge for up to 12 hours, but it is not suitable for freezing).

Bake the torte in the pre-heated oven for about 30 minutes, until golden brown and the sponge springs back when pressed.

Serve the torte warm with cream, ice cream or classic custard. If you have any spare plums, remove the stones, gently soften by cooking for 2-3 mins and purée. Serve as a sauce poured over the torte.

Lizzie Yell

Mincemeat Streusel

This recipe is very quick and easy. It takes a long time to make mince pies, lots of rolling and cutting out when there is so much to do at Christmas. We find it far quicker to make one large one and then cut it into pieces. A great plus point is that you get more mincemeat too. The cooked streusel freezes very well. Always serve warm with cream or brandy butter.

 Serves 16 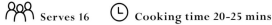 **Cooking time 20-25 mins**

Ingredients:

Pastry

175g plain white flour

1½ tbsp icing sugar, sifted

100g butter

a little cold water

Filling

450g mincemeat

Topping

75g butter

75g self-raising white flour

40g semolina

40g caster sugar

Method

Pre-heat the oven to 200C.

You will need a 23 x 33 cm Swiss roll tin or small roasting tin, lightly greased

Measure the flour and icing sugar into a mixing bowl and rub in the butter until the mixture resembles coarse breadcrumbs. Add just sufficient water to mix to a firm dough. If you prefer, this can be made in a processor. If time allows wrap the dough in cling film and chill for about 30 mins. Roll out the pastry to a rectangle slightly larger than the tin, then line the base and sides of the tin with pastry. Trim the pastry level with the top edges of the tin and patch any gaps if necessary. Spread the mincemeat evenly over the pastry base.

To make the topping, melt the butter and allow to cool slightly. Pour onto the remaining topping ingredients into a bowl and mix together until it combines to form a dough. If you have time chill the dough as this makes grating easier. Using a coarse grater grate the topping over the mincemeat and spread evenly.

Bake in a pre-heated oven for about 20-25 minutes until golden brown.

Divide the streusel into slices, it makes about 16 slices, and dust with icing sugar. Serve warm with cream or brandy butter.

The slices of streusel can be frozen, thawed and warmed in a pre-heated oven at 150C for about 20 minutes. Dust with icing sugar before serving.

Mary Berry - Chef

Melinda Pudding

My boys adore this indulgent syrupy pudding which can be served with custard, cream or ice-cream. It was given to me by my South African friend and is the family favourite.

 Serves 10    **Preparation time 10 mins**   **Cooking time 25 mins**

Ingredients:

Pudding

2 cups self-raising flour

2 level tsp bicarbonate of soda

1½ cups brown sugar

2 eggs

1 tin (14oz) of fruit cocktail
    with syrup

Syrup

1 cup granulated sugar

1 small tin carnation milk
    (evaporated milk)

4 tbsp butter

dash of vanilla essence

Method

Pre-heat the oven to 180C.

This recipe requires a 12 inch flan dish. A shallow pie dish can also be used.

In a large mixing bowl combine all the pudding ingredients together. Pour into the dish. Bake in the oven for 30 minutes or until firm to touch like a sponge would be.

While the pudding is baking prepare the syrup. Put all the ingredients in a saucepan and melt on a low heat stirring until everything is dissolved.

As the pudding comes out of the oven, prick it all over with a fork and pour the syrup all over the pudding immediately. It doesn't matter if some of it settles on top. Leave to stand to absorb the syrup.

Either keep warm until needed or cool and reheat later. Cut into slices and serve from the dish.

Heather Hiscox

Quince and Queen Pudding

They say the French cook with love, Italians with flair, Spanish with passion, Germans with their belly and the British with their wallet; certainly the case with our puddings, stale bread features in many classic British Puds. Bread and butter pudding, summer pudding, Diplomat pudding, apple charlotte and the following Queen of Pudding recipe.

I've added quince to this favourite old Mrs Beeton recipe. Quince, a yellow pear shaped fruit with the most incredible perfume when in season. It is hard and bitter when raw so requires cooking.

 Serves 10    **Preparation time 10 mins**   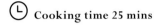 **Cooking time 25 mins**

Ingredients:

1 quince

grated zest and juice of one lime

75g butter

290mls milk

140g caster sugar

60g fresh white breadcrumbs

grated zest of one lemon

2 eggs, separated

2 tbsp good fruit compote or preserve, such as straw berry, raspberry or damson

thick cream to serve.

Method

Pre-heat the oven to 180C.

Peel and core the quince then cut it into 1cm cubes. In a small pan, melt 50g of the butter. Add the quince, lime zest and juice and cook, stirring occasionally until the quince is softened and lightly coloured. Cool, then drain the quince and pat dry on kitchen paper. Set aside.

Heat the milk and add the remaining butter with 30g of the sugar. Stir until the sugar dissolves, then add the breadcrumbs and lemon zest. Remove from the heat and allow to cool. Stir the egg yolks into the breadcrumb mixture. Stir in the quince and pour the mixture into a 600ml pie dish. Leave to stand for 30 minutes.

Pre-heat the oven to 180C.

Place the dish in a roasting tin and pour hot water into the tin to come about two thirds of the way up the outside of the dish. Bake the pudding for 45 minutes or until it is just set. Allow to cool slightly.

Reduce the oven temperature to 150C.

Warm the fruit compote or preserve and carefully spread over the pudding.

Whisk the egg whites until stiff. Whisk in 2 tablespoons of the remaining sugar. Whisk again until very stiff and shiny, then fold in all but a half-tablespoon of the remaining sugar. Pipe the meringue on top of the pudding and dust the top lightly with the reserved sugar. Bake for about 10 minutes, until the meringue is set and pale golden.

Serve hot, with thick cream.

Paul Clerehugh - Chef

Cold puddings

Quick Lemon and Lime Cheesecake

A quick and easy dessert that is full of flavour.

 Serves 6-8   **Preparation time 20 mins**   **Chilling time 2 hrs**

Ingredients:

200g digestive biscuits

50g melted butter

1 x 397mls tin of condensed milk

150mls pint double cream

zest and juice of 2 lemons and 2 limes

Method

Whizz the biscuits in a food processor or crush them in a plastic bag with a rolling pin. Add the melted butter, mix well and press into the base of a 9in flan ring. Chill in the fridge.

Pour the condensed milk into a bowl and whisk in the cream. Gently whisk in the zest and juice of the lemons and limes, until the mixture is smooth.

Pour the mixture into the crumb base and leave to set in the fridge. This will take about two hours.

Laura Mayes

Rhubarb and Ginger Cheesecake

This is one of my favourite desserts given to me by a like-minded "foodie" friend. The combination of rhubarb and ginger is just delicious!

 Serves 8    **Preparation time 20 mins**   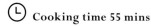 **Cooking time 55 mins**

Ingredients:

500g rhubarb

1 piece of Chinese stem ginger in syrup, finely chopped, plus 2 tbsp syrup from the jar

175g caster sugar

175g digestive biscuits

50g butter, melted

2 x 250g tubs mascarpone cheese

2 tbsp cornflour

3 large eggs

Method

Pre-heat the oven to 180C.

Line the base of a 23cm round spring-form cake tin with baking parchment.

Roughly chop the rhubarb into 2cm pieces and place in a saucepan with the stem ginger, syrup, 100g of the caster sugar and 4 tbsp of water. Poach for 10 minutes until the rhubarb is tender. Tip the cooked rhubarb into a sieve over a bowl and strain. Reserve the juices.

Crush the biscuits in a large plastic bag with a rolling pin. Tip into a bowl and stir in the melted butter. Place the crumb mixture in the cake tin, pressing down firmly with the back of a spoon. Chill in the fridge.

Using an electric whisk, beat together the mascarpone, cornflour, eggs and remaining 75g sugar for 1-2 minutes until smooth. Spoon the strained rhubarb in the mascarpone mixture and gently swirl, taking care not to over mix. Pour in the cake tin and bake for 45 minutes, or until golden and firm.

Leave to cool before removing from the tin.

Cut into wedges and serve drizzled with the reserved rhubarb syrup. Dust with icing sugar.

Maria Lockhart

White Chocolate and Toblerone Cheesecake with Summer Berries

I have been making this indulgent cheesecake for years, and it doesn't seem to have lost any of its appeal. You need to make sure you have a deep tin as there is a lot of filling. It looks great decorated with a selection of berries such as raspberries, redcurrants, and blackberries. The sharpness of the berries works really well with the rich cheesecake.

 Serves 8    Prep time 30 mins   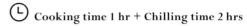 Cooking time 1 hr + Chilling time 2 hrs

Ingredients:

150g digestive biscuits

75g butter, melted

800g cream cheese

50g mascarpone

6 eggs

200g caster sugar

350g white chocolate

1 small bar of Toblerone, broken into small pieces

summer berries (to decorate)

Method

Pre-heat the oven to 180C.

Crush the biscuits in a large plastic bag with a rolling pin or in a food processor. Tip into a bowl and add the melted butter.

Line the bottom of a deep 20cm (8 inch) spring form tin, pressing the crumbs down with your hands or the back of a spoon. Chill in the fridge for 30 mins.

Break the white chocolate into a bowl and melt gently over a saucepan of barely simmering water.

Place the cream cheese, mascarpone, eggs, sugar and white chocolate in a food processor and blend until creamy.

Line the outside of the chilled tin with foil so that it covers the bottom and sides in one large piece. (This protects the cheesecake from the water as it is cooked in a water bath).

Pour the filling over the biscuit base and sprinkle the toblerone on top. Tap gently so the pieces sink.

Create a bain marie by putting the tin in a roasting dish and pouring hot water from a recently boiled kettle around the cheesecake, to about halfway up the tin.

Bake in the oven for about 1 hour. The centre should be just set on top but slightly wobbly underneath.

Turn off the oven and leave the cheesecake inside to cool with the door ajar for 30 mins.

Refrigerate for at least 2 hours.

Decorate with summer berries and dust with icing sugar just before serving.

Nicola Williams

Chocolate Cheesecake

This is a retro classic and takes me back to the '80s when cheesecloth shirts and cheesecakes were all the rage! As I love chocolate this makes a lovely change from the traditional cheesecake.

 Serves 8    **Preparation time 20 mins**   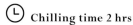 **Chilling time 2 hrs**

Ingredients:

50g butter, melted

150g digestive biscuits, finely crushed

175g plain chocolate

225g cream cheese

75g caster sugar

2 eggs, separated

300mls double cream, whipped

chocolate curls to decorate

Method

You will need a 23cm spring-form tin or flan dish.

First make the cheesecake base by combining the melted butter and biscuit crumbs and press the mixture into the spring form tin. Place in the fridge.

To make the cheesecake, melt the chocolate in a bowl over a pan of hot water.

In a separate bowl blend the cream cheese, caster sugar and egg yolks until smooth. Now mix in the chocolate. Whip 150mls of cream until thick and fold into the chocolate mixture.

In a clean bowl, whisk the egg whites until stiff and fold carefully into the chocolate mixture. Turn the mixture into the spring form tin and place in the fridge to set.

Once set, whip the remaining 150mls of cream, place in a piping bag if you have one, and use to decorate the cheesecake. Sprinkle with chocolate curls. Carefully remove from the spring form tin and serve.

Juliet Baxter

Chocolate Marquise

This chocolate dessert is so easy to make and freezes beautifully. It can be sliced and served directly from the freezer and so makes for a great standby when time is short, or friends call in unexpectedly. It has come to my rescue many times including the odd occasion when I've needed a chocolate fix.

 **Serves 10-12**　　 **Preparation time 20 mins**　　 **Chilling time 12 hrs**

Ingredients:

400g good quality 70% dark
　　chocolate

6 egg yolks

150g caster sugar

150g unsalted butter softened

4 tbsp cocoa powder sifted

2 tbsp strong coffee

300mls double cream, lightly
　　whipped

6 tbsp brandy or to taste

200g fresh raspberries

Method

You will need a 1kg loaf tin lined with cling film.

Melt the chocolate over a pan of boiling water without stirring.

In a clean bowl beat the egg yolks with 75g sugar until pale.

In a separate bowl, cream together the softened butter with the remaining 75g sugar until light and no longer granular. Mix in the cocoa powder.

Pour the melted chocolate into the softened butter, add the egg mix, the whipped cream, the coffee and the brandy and fold together until thoroughly combined.

Pour mixture into prepared loaf tin and chill overnight.

Serve with fresh raspberries and pouring cream.

Julia Francisco

Passion Fruit and White Chocolate Pots

These Passion Fruit Pots are great as they can be made in advance, the day before even, taking the pressure off doing all the cooking at once. Who can resist either white chocolate or passion fruit, and they are even more irresistible together!

Serves 12   **Preparation time 20 mins**   **Chilling time 3 hrs**

Ingredients:

12 ripe passion fruits

2 tbsp lemon juice

600mls double cream

100g caster sugar

150g organic white chocolate

Method

Scoop the pulp from 10 of the passion fruits into a food processor or blender. Add the lemon juice and blitz for 10 seconds. Tip into a sieve over a bowl and rub the juice and pulp through with a spatula. Remembering to scrape of any purée from the bottom of the sieve.

Put the cream, sugar and chocolate in a small saucepan and heat very gently, stirring often, until completely melted and smooth.

Add the sieved juice and pulp and stir in well. Pour into the espresso cup or ramekins and chill for at least 3 hours until set.

To serve, scrape the pulp from the remaining passion fruits and top each pot with ½ tsp of the seeds and juice.

Lucy Montgomery

Passion Fruit and White Chocolate Pots   **145**

Stephen's Crème Brûlée with Blueberries

I fell in love with Crème Brûlée when celebrating my parents Silver Wedding anniversary at The Elizabeth Restaurant in Oxford more than 30 years ago. Since undergraduate days I have been trying to emulate what I experienced that evening. Over time I have tried a number of variations on the theme and find that the most popular is when the intense vanilla and cream is cut with blueberries.

 Serves 6   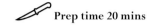 **Prep time 20 mins**   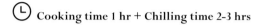 **Cooking time 1 hr + Chilling time 2-3 hrs**

Ingredients:

6 egg yolks

4 oz sugar (caster or granulated – makes no difference)

1 pint single cream

1 vanilla pod – NOT essence!

1 small packet of blueberries

demerara sugar for the Brûlée

Method

Pre-heat the oven to 150C.

Separate the egg yolks from their whites and place the yolks in a large bowl. Add the sugar to the yolks and blend thoroughly with a spoon.

Pour the cream into a saucepan. Slice the vanilla pod along its length and strip out the seeds. Put the seeds and the pod into the cream. Heat gently, to bring the cream almost to the boil but not to boiling.

Pour the near boiling cream and vanilla pod onto the egg and sugar mixture and stir vigorously. Sieve the mixture into a large jug.

Place 6 ramekin dishes into a deep roasting tray. Place about 6-8 blueberries into each ramekin. Pour the sieved mixture into each ramekin on top of the blueberries and fill to as near the lip as possible. You need to keep stirring the custard otherwise all the vanilla seeds will go to the bottom of the jug!

Pour cold water into the roasting tray to create a "Bain Marie" until the cold water reaches about ¾ of the way up the side of the ramekins.

Bake in the oven for 1 to 1.5 hours. Remove and allow to cool, then chill (the blueberries should rise to the surface!).

1 hour before serving put 1 small teaspoonful of Demerara sugar onto each dessert and spread out evenly. Either put the ramekins under a very hot grill or blow torch the sugar until it is melted and almost burning. This cannot be achieved in an Aga! Again allow to cool before putting the dishes in a fridge until pudding is served.

Stephen Richards

Greek Yogurt Pannacottas with Rhubarb Compote

Little creamy wobbling jellies with deep-pink rhubarb and green pistachios: this comforting food just makes you want to smile. I love traditional pannacottas, but unfortunately they are usually made with double cream, sugar and rum, and although sometimes it feels like happiness can be found at the bottom of a cream pie, it doesn't help.

My pannacottas are made with wonderful Greek yogurt and natural honey, and so are better for you (the yogurt and honey both contain healthy bacteria) but still taste delicious. Don't be put off by the setting time: a little pre-planning goes a long way and, after all, anticipation is part of the joy of eating!

 Serves 4    **Prep time 15 mins**   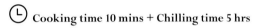 **Cooking time 10 mins + Chilling time 5 hrs**

Ingredients:

Panacotta

4 sheets leaf gelatine

200mls milk

1 vanilla pod

2 tbsp runny honey

250g tub 0% fat Greek yogurt

Compote

200g pink rhubarb

75g fruit sugar, such as
   Fruisana, or 100g caster
   sugar

1 tbsp chopped pistachios

Method

First, to make the pannacottas, put the gelatine into a bowl and cover with cold water, then leave to one side until it becomes floppy.

Pour the milk into a saucepan and heat gently. Slit the vanilla pod on one side and open it up. Using the tip of a sharp knife, scrape out the sticky seeds and add to the milk with the empty pod and the honey. Bring gently to the boil and remove from the heat when it starts to bubble around the pan sides.

Drain off the gelatine sheets, squeezing out any excess water and stir into the hot milk until dissolved. Then beat in the yogurt until smooth and pour through a sieve into a bowl.

You can pour the mix into moulds now, but the vanilla seeds will sink to the bottom. So I prefer allowing the mixture to cool then chilling it in the fridge, stirring every 30 minutes or so, until it begins to set around the edges. As the mixture thickens you

can then decant it into 4 lightly oiled, round metal moulds (of about 125ml capacity) or ramekins. Then chill for about 3 hours until completely set. While the pannacottas are chilling, make the compote. Trim the rhubarb and cut into 3cm lengths. Heat the sugar with 100mls of water in a medium saucepan, stirring until dissolved. Add the rhubarb and bring to the boil. Simmer very gently for about 5 minutes, trying to keep the rhubarb pieces intact if possible. Remove and leave to cool.

When the compote is cooled, run a table knife around the panna-cottas, shake out on to small dessert plates and serve the compote alongside. Sprinkle with the pistachios and serve.

Sophie Mitchell - Chef

Ginger, Pear and Molasses Trifle

This is another recipe from my teenage experiments. I think that the first "custard base" was far less salubrious than the more refined version below, from memory it was just a sweet white sauce made with molasses sugar and finished with cream. Actually it was delicious and one of those recipes that I have been meaning to resurrect and refine for years and somehow never got around to. This book has lent me the perfect excuse and it is now very much part of my repertoire.

 Serves 6-8   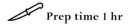 **Prep time 1 hr**   **Cooking time 1 hr + Chilling time 2 hrs**

Ingredients:

Ginger cake (best made the day before)

175g soft butter

175g soft dark brown sugar

100g golden syrup

75g black treacle

200mls milk

2 large eggs, beaten

325g self-raising flour

2 tsp ground ginger

1 ½ tsp bicarbonate of soda

Trifle

1/3 to a 1/2 of the above cake or a shop bought Jamaican ginger cake, sliced

1x 450g tin of pear quarters in juice, strained and juice reserved

300mls double cream

200mls milk

3 egg yolks

2 tbsp or 30g molasses cane sugar

¼ tsp salt

1 tsp corn flour

2 stem ginger rounds, finely diced

3 tbsp of the stem ginger syrup and

3 tbsp of the reserved pear juice

Method

Pre-heat the oven to 150C.

Line the base of a deep 22cm square cake tin with greaseproof paper.

To make the cake, put the butter, sugar, syrup and treacle into a large pan (one which can contain the entire cake mixture) and gently heat until everything is melted. Do not allow the mixture to get too hot. Remove the pan from the heat and whisk in the milk and the eggs. Add the flour and bicarbonate of soda and stir the mixture gently until mixed.

Pour the mixture into the prepared cake tin and bake in the oven for 1 hour, until the cake begins to pull away from the sides of the tin and is firm to touch. Remove from the oven. Leave to cool for ten minutes before turning out onto a cooling wire. Once cooled wrap well and store for 2-3 days before using. This develops the flavour and a slightly sticky texture.

To make the trifle, cut the cake into slices. Take a pretty 1 litre serving bowl and arrange the cake slices on the base and about 1/2 of the way up the sides. Scatter in the pear quarters (you can chop these into chunks if preferred) and then sprinkle over 100mls of the reserved pear juice.

To make the molasses custard, put the milk and 100mls of cream into a small pan and bring to scalding point.

Put the egg yolks along with the molasses sugar, salt and corn flour into a heat proof mixing bowl and blend well together, pressing out any lumps in the sugar.

When the milk is at scalding point pour it over the egg yolk mix and blend well. Pour the mixture back into the pan and over a medium low heat stir until the mixture thickens and begins to bubble. Do not be tempted to speed this process up or the eggs will scramble.

Method - Continued...

When the custard is cooked pour it over the cake and pears in the serving dish. Cover and set aside to cool.

To make the syllabub topping, pour the remaining 200mls of cream into a mixing bowl and add 3 tablespoons of the ginger syrup and 3 tablespoons of the pear juice. Whisk together until the cream thickens to form soft peaks which gently hold their shape. Fold in the finely chopped stem ginger.

Spoon the ginger cream over the custard and refrigerate until required.

Delicious served with ginger Florentine biscuits.

Belinda Hill - Stirring Stuff Cookery School

Christmas Tiramisu

This is a great pudding that is made the day before and is a good alternative to traditional Christmas puddings. But don't think it is only for Christmas. It is a refreshing dessert that can be made at any time of the year with any berries that are available.

 Serves 6-8 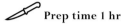 **Prep time 1 hr**   **Cooking time 1 hr + Chilling time 2 hrs**

Ingredients:

800g frozen mixed berries

350g caster sugar

1 tbsp Creme de Cassis

3 eggs separated

450g mascarpone

1 tsp vanilla essence

pinch of salt

Savoiardi biscuits/sponge fingers

50g dark chocolate, grated

Method

Put the frozen fruit and 210g of the caster sugar into a large pan and heat gently. Simmer for 10 minutes. Strain the fruit reserving the syrup. Stir the cassis into the syrup.

In a large bowl whisk the egg yolks and the remaining sugar (140g) until the mixture is pale and full of volume. Whisk in the mascarpone and add the vanilla essence. In a separate bowl, whisk the egg whites with a pinch of salt until they form soft peaks. Fold the egg whites into the mascarpone mixture.

Dip the biscuits into the syrup, soak them well and lay them in the base of the dish you are using. Spread half the cheese mixture over the biscuits, covering them well. Then spread over half the fruit. Dip the remaining biscuits in the syrup and arrange on top of this fruit mixture, then cover with the remaining fruit. Finally cover everything with the remaining cheese mixture.

Cover and chill overnight.

Garnish with grated chocolate before serving.

Use left over syrup as a pouring sauce

Emma Marshall

Not Your Average Tiramisu

The original format of this recipe was given to me by my friend Lindi back in the early 90's before Tiramisu really took off and became a supermarket and gastropub favourite. I have adapted it over the years and she would hardly recognise or perhaps even remember this recipe. It has always proved an outstanding pudding with friends and family and I will ensure Lindi receives a copy of the book at Christmas!

 Serves 12    **Preparation time 20 mins**   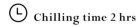 **Chilling time 2 hrs**

Ingredients:

5 small (250g) tubs mascarpone cheese

7 egg yolks

7 tsp vanilla sugar

7 tbsp icing sugar

150mls cold espresso coffee

3 tbsp Tia Maria

approx 350g – 400g medium Amaretti biscuits, not individually wrapped variety

cocoa powder to dust

Method

Use a simple straight sided shallow glass bowl (approx 3 inches high by 10-12 inches if possible) but a trifle dish would work too.

Blend together the egg yolks and sugars with electric whisk. Fold in the mascarpone cheese, use an electric whisk on pulse to assist if cheese is quite firm. It is important not to over blend the mixture as it will become too liquid.

Mix the coffee and Tia Maria in small bowl. Dip the amaretti biscuits into the coffee mixture one at a time for a few seconds, until they absorb the liquid but do not break up. Spread the dipped amaretti across bottom of dish and then layer with half of the cheese mixture. Repeat layers again and finally dust with cocoa powder.

Louise Turrill

Quick Lemon Soufflé

This is the perfect party pudding served with meringues. It takes me back to when I was a child as my Irish grandmother used to make it. It is incredibly light and refreshing.

 Serves 6-8    **Preparation time 20 mins**   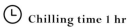 **Chilling time 1 hr**

Ingredients:

3 eggs, separated

110g caster sugar

15g powered gelatine

1 lemon

250mls double cream,
   whipped

Method

In a large bowl, cream the egg yolks, sugar and lemon rind together. Slowly add the lemon juice and beat until thick.

Dissolve the gelatine in water according to the instructions on the packet. Fold into the egg yolk mixture.

Fold in the whipped cream.

Whisk the egg whites until they form soft peaks, and fold into the mixture. Transfer to a pretty glass serving dish or 6 individual scrving dishes and chill in the fridge.

Vivi Blount

Gatêau Diane

Laziness is the mother of invention! Or at least I am sure that is how this particular recipe came into being. Cooking for over 120 guests for my 18th birthday party, I decided that it was far too complicated to make this cake in the traditional manner. It was much easier to just crush the meringues into the chocolate ganache and tip the whole lot into a cake tin to set. Being contrary, I then spent hours making the perfect marzipan roses to decorate! The end result was both delicious and beautiful.

 **Serves 10-12**   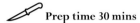 **Prep time 30 mins**   **Chilling time 2 hrs (preferably overnight)**

Ingredients:

1 tub mini meringues (16 meringue pack size)

100g very dark chocolate, either Willies Venezuelan Black or Lindt excellent 90%

2 egg whites

100g icing sugar

225g good quality salted butter, softened

2 tbsp orange blossom honey

Method

Grate or break the chocolate into pieces and put into a heatproof bowl placed over a pan of simmering water. Stir occasionally and once melted remove from the heat and allow to cool.

Cut the softened butter into pieces and put into a large mixing bowl along with the honey. Beat well with an electric mixer until the mixture is soft and light. Set aside until required.

Put the egg whites and the icing sugar into a large mixing bowl and place this over a pan of simmering water. Whisk until the mixture is meringue like, shiny and holding its shape well. Remove from the heat and allow this mixture to cool before combining the prepared ingredients.

Whilst the component parts are cooling line a 20cm loose based shallow cake tin with cling film and crush the meringues into a bowl. You need a bit of texture so be careful not to crush too finely. I find they break quite happily when crushed with one hand.

Once the chocolate and the meringue are cooled sufficiently to prevent the butter from melting combine the ingredients. Using a spatula fold the meringue mixture into the butter along with the cooled melted chocolate. Finally stir in the crushed meringue.

Spoon the mixture into the prepared tin and spread evenly. Refrigerated for at least 2 hours and preferably over night.

To serve remove the cake from the tin and remove the cling film. Place on a serving plate and dredge with cocoa powder. If serving the cake whole you might decorate with fresh roses. To serve in individual portions cut into thin slices and place on to the dessert plates along with either a fresh orange and Grand Marnier salad or a dark berry or cherry compote.

Belinda Hill - Stirring Stuff Cookery School

Danish Strawberry Shortcake

This is a really pretty dessert with layers of cake, cream and strawberries – perfect for summer entertaining.

Serves 8   **Preparation time 25 mins**   **Cooking time 15 mins**

Ingredients:

Shortcake

175g butter

175g caster sugar

2 eggs

175g self-raising flour, sifted

2 level tsp ground cinnamon

Filling

450g fresh strawberries,
    hulled

300mls double cream

icing sugar to dust

Method

Pre-heat the oven to 160C.

Lightly grease and line three 18cm round cake tins.

Cream the butter and sugar until light and fluffy. Beat in the eggs one at a time and then fold in the sifted flour and cinnamon. Divide the mixture between the 3 tins and bake in the oven for 15 minutes. Leave to cool completely.

Once the shortcake has cooled, chop ¾ of the strawberries into small pieces and whip the cream. Gently mix 2/3 of the whipped cream with the chopped strawberries, leaving enough cream to decorate the top of the gateaux. Sandwich the 3 layers of shortcake together with the cream and strawberry mixture.

Top with the remaining cream and decorate with the halved or sliced strawberries. Dust with icing sugar just before serving.

Hazel Hawkes

Danish Strawberry Shortcake

Raspberry and Hazelnut Roulade with Apricot and Grand Marnier Coulis

An impressive and fairly simple pudding to create and always an absolute hit!

 Serves 8-10   **Preparation time 30 mins**   **Cooking time 15 mins**

Ingredients:

Roulade

170g chopped hazelnuts

115g caster sugar

4 eggs, separated

300mls double cream

2 punnets of fresh raspberries

Icing sugar

Coulis

1 tin of apricots in fruit juice

A jolly good splash of Grand Marnier!

Decoration

8-10 sprigs of fresh mint

Method

Pre-heat the oven to 170C.

Line a 38cm x 38cm swiss roll tin with baking paper.

Whisk together the egg yolks and caster sugar with an electric mixer until pale and thick. Fold in the chopped hazelnuts.

Whisk the egg whites to form soft peaks. Gently fold into the egg yolks. Pour into the swiss roll tin and bake in the oven for about 15 minutes until slightly golden and spongy to touch. Remove from oven and cool.

Turn the roulade upside down onto another similar sized piece of baking paper, which has been generously dusted with icing sugar, and carefully remove the baking paper from the base of the roulade.

Softly whip the double cream and spread evenly over the roulade. Sprinkle with fresh raspberries. With the wider edge in front of you, carefully roll the roulade up and twist the ends of the baking paper to form a tight roll. Chill in the fridge.

To make the coulis simply whiz together the apricots (with juice) and Grand Marnier in a liquidiser until smooth.

To serve, cut the roulade into slices. If you have an electric knife, this is excellent for achieving a sharp, neat slice, otherwise use a sharp chef's knife. Spoon a little coulis onto each pudding plate and by using the back of the spoon, make a neat circle with it. Top each with a roulade slice and sprig of mint and serve.

The roulade can be made up to a day in advance. Once cooled top with damp kitchen roll and wrap in cling film. Keep in a cool place.

Camilla Skinner

Lemon Tart

 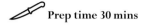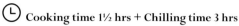
Ingredients:

Pastry

150g unsalted butter

90g caster sugar

1 medium egg

225g plain sifted flour

1 tbsp cold water

Filling

75g dark chocolate, 70%
   cocoa solids

6 egg yolks

3 eggs

275g caster sugar

500mls double cream

zest and juice from 3 lemons

icing sugar for presentation

Method

Make the pastry by blitzing the butter and sugar in a food processor, add the egg and blitz for 30 seconds. Add the flour and blitz until the mixture forms dough. If necessary add a little cold water. Remove from the processor and gently knead to form a ball. Cover with cling film and chill for 2 hours.

Set the oven to 190C. Roll out the pastry and line a 26cm loose bottomed, lightly greased tart ring. Chill for 30 minutes and then line the ring with baking parchment and baking beans. Cook for 15 to 20 minutes until the edges begin to colour. Remove from the oven and take out the baking beans and parchment. Return to the oven and bake for a further 10 minutes until the base is cooked.

Meanwhile melt the chocolate gently in a glass bowl over a pan of boiling water. Allow to cool and then brush the base of the tart with the melted chocolate.

Reset the oven to 170C.

Whisk the egg yolks, eggs and sugar together and slowly stir in the cream. Slowly add the lemon juice and zest to thicken the cream.

Strain the filling into a jug and add half the mixture to the pastry case. Place on the bottom shelf of the oven, pull the shelf half way out and add the remainder of the mixture. Place back into the oven and bake for about 60 to 70 minutes until the filling is just set.

Remove from the oven and allow to cool. Remove from the flan ring, and leave to cool. Dust with icing sugar and using a cook's blow torch to caramelise the top.

Kevin Woodford - Chef

Lemon Meringue Ice Cream

This is very easy and quick to make, and there is no need for an ice cream maker. Serve it with a fruit coulis for a dinner party or on its own when you get caught short for a pudding.

 Serves 8   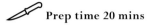 **Prep time 20 mins**   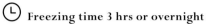 **Freezing time 3 hrs or overnight**

Ingredients:

570mls whipping cream

225g Greek yoghurt

5 meringue nests (bought ones are fine)

320g good quality lemon curd

juice & rind of 1 lemon

Method

Whip the cream until fairly stiff and fold in the yoghurt. Add the lemon curd, lemon juice and zest. Roughly break up the meringue nests and add to the mixture. Put into a rectangular Tupperware box and freeze.

To serve – Take out of the freezer about 15 minutes before you need it and serve sliced with a couple of mint leaves for decoration or a red fruit coulis.

Tessa Rose

Lemon Ice Cream

This tastes sophisticated and is in fact very simple to make. Delicious with a fresh raspberry sauce

 **Serves 8-10**    **Preparation time 10 mins**   **Freezing time 12 hrs**

Ingredients:

600mls double cream

450g caster sugar

600mls full fat milk

5-6 lemons

Method

Mix together the cream, sugar and milk plus the grated zest of the lemons. Freeze.

The next day, defrost the frozen mixture until soft enough to mix in the juice of the lemons. Refreeze. No churning needed.

Take out of the freezer about 10 minutes before serving to soften slightly.

Kate Sloane

The Ultimate Strawberry Tart

 Serves 6    **Preparation time 30 mins**   **Cooking time 15 mins**

Ingredients:

Tart

280g puff pastry

450g cream cheese

450g strawberries, hulled

4 passion fruit

icing sugar to taste

Glaze

5 tbsp redcurrant jelly and a
*   splash water*

Method

Pre-heat the oven to 200C.

On a lightly floured surface, roll out the pastry to form a rectangle approx. 35cm x 14cm. Using a knife mark a picture frame style border around the pastry, making sure not to cut all the way through. Prick the inside of the border, liberally, with a fork. Place on a baking tray and allow to rest in the fridge for 20 minutes. Bake for 10-15 minutes or until cooked. If the centre rises up, gently push down with a fish slice.

Beat the cream cheese with the passion fruit until soft and creamy and sweeten with a little icing sugar to taste. Beat in a splash of water if the cheese mix is too stiff and pile the mixture into the cooled pastry case, levelling off with a round bladed knife.

Heat the redcurrant jelly in a pan with the water until smooth. Remove from the heat and strain through a sieve to remove any lumps. Set to one side to cool slightly.

Arrange the strawberries over the passion fruit cream and cover with the redcurrant glaze.

Lesley Waters - Chef

Black Bottom Pudding

My mother-in-law served this pudding the very first time my husband took me home to meet his parents and I was so impressed I asked her for the recipe. The recipe was from her mother, who had discovered it on a visit to Hawaii. The Japanese were not her favourite people, as one of her sons had been a prisoner of war and had worked on the infamous Burma railway. However whilst on holiday in Hawaii after the war, she was invited to dinner at the home of a Japanese family and this dessert was served!

 Serves 6-8    **Preparation time 35 mins**    **Chilling time 1 hr**

Ingredients:

18 ginger biscuit

50g butter

4 eggs

1 tbsp cornflour

½ cup white sugar

500mls full fat milk

50g good quality plain
    chocolate

1 sachet of powdered gelatine

3 tbsp rum

1 tsp vanilla extract

300mls double cream

Method

Pre-heat the oven to 160C.

Melt the butter. Crush the biscuits in a plastic bag with a rolling pin or in a food processor. Add to the melted butter. Press into the base of a 20 cm flan dish and chill in the fridge.

Separate the egg yolks from the whites. Combine the yolks with the cornflour, sugar and a little milk to make a paste. Warm the rest of the milk and pour over the yolk mixture. Return the mixture to the pan and gently heat until the custard thickens.

Put the chocolate in a heat proof bowl and gently melt over a pan of barely simmering water. Add a cup of custard to the melted chocolate. Cool, then pour over the biscuit base.

Soak the gelatine in 2 tablespoons of water and heat gently till melted.

Add the gelatine to the remaining custard and mix well. Allow to cool. When beginning to set add the rum and vanilla extract.

Whisk egg whites until they form soft peaks. Fold the egg whites into the setting custard and pile onto the chocolate layer.

Before serving whisk up the double cream and pile on top of the custard, decorate with grated chocolate.

Sue Bayfield

Mojito Ice Cream

I came up with this recipe after our summer holiday in Greece. Every evening we would leave the beach to sip ice cold Mojito Cocktails at the beach bar. Mojitos are traditional Cuban cocktails made with white rum, mint, sugar and lime juice.

The flavour of this ice cream can be adapted by using different spirits. For Margarita ice cream use Tequila and Triple Sec. For Cointreau ice cream use Tequila and Cointreau and substitute the juice of 4 of the limes for the juice of 2 oranges.

 Serves 8    Preparation time 20 mins    Freezing time 12 hrs

Ingredients:

375mls double cream

6 egg yolks

397g tin sweetened condensed milk

120mls white rum

juice of 6 limes

zest of 1 lime

4 tsp of fresh mint very finely chopped

Method

Put the cream into a saucepan and heat gently until almost boiling.

Whisk the egg yolks in a bowl. Add the warm cream and continue whisking. Return the mixture to the saucepan and cook gently, stirring all the time, until the custard thickens. Pour it into a clean bowl to cool.

Add the condensed milk, rum, lime juice, zest and mint and mix well.

Put the mixture into an ice cream maker if you have one and freeze. If not, put into a lidded container in the freezer. Remove the ice cream every hour over the next three hours and beat with an electric whisk to remove any ice crystals. Return to the freezer until needed.

Take the ice cream out of the freezer 15 minutes before serving to soften.

Nicola Williams

Raspberry and Blackcurrant Sorbet

This is an easy sorbet recipe that can be made with a combination of any red fruits depending on what is available. It is a now a tradition that we have raspberry sorbet on Christmas Eve.

 Serves 4   Preparation time 20 mins

Ingredients:

500g fruit

150-200 g caster sugar

juice of 1 lemon

Method

In a food processor, purée the fruit, sugar and lemon juice. Put through a sieve and then into an ice cream maker until frozen. Eat within 24 hours.

Kate Sloane

Easy Vanilla Ice Cream

This ice cream really is very quick and easy to make with no stirring necessary and it tastes really delicious. It is made in a loaf tin which can then be turned out to reveal a beautifully decorated top before slicing to serve.

 Serves 6-8   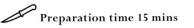 Preparation time 15 mins   Freezing time 12 hrs

Ingredients:

Ice cream

2 eggs, separated

600mls double cream

125g icing sugar, sifted

scraped vanilla pod or 2 tsp
vanilla extract

Decorating options

50g-75g chocolate and fudge
chunks

100g sliced fruit

favourite sweets

Method

Line a 1kg loaf tin with plenty of cling film and decorate the base with any of the decorating options.

Separate the eggs and whisk the egg whites into stiff peaks.

In a separate bowl, whisk the cream, sugar and vanilla into soft peaks (there is no need to wash the whisk if done in this order).

In a 3rd bowl beat the egg yolks until pale and creamy. Stir the egg yolks into the cream mixture, then gently fold in the egg whites.

Carefully pour the mixture into the prepared tin. Pull the spare cling film over the top and freeze for 12 hours. There is no need to stir!

10 minutes before serving, turn out ready for slicing.

Lisa Perkins

Ice Cream Cake

This is a different, light and easy dessert to make. I make it for supper parties or for family lunches as the kids love it.

 Serves 8   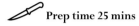 Prep time 25 mins   Cooking time 40 mins + Freezing time 2-3 hrs

Ingredients:

Base

5 egg whites

200g caster sugar

200g ground almonds

2 tsp baking powder

Topping

5 egg yolks

100g caster sugar

300mls whipping cream

2 tbsp strong coffee or 1 tsp vanilla extract

fruits or chocolates of your choice to decorate

Method

Pre-heat the oven to 160C.

To make the base, whisk the egg whites until it forms stiff peaks, gradually add the sugar and continue whisking until glossy. Mix the ground almond with the baking powder and fold into the whisked egg whites. Put mixture in 24cm round baking tin with removable base. Cook in the middle of the oven for 40 minutes. Leave to cool completely.

To make the ice cream, whisk the egg yolks with the sugar until pale and stiff. Whisk the cream and add to the egg yolk mix. Add the coffee. Add the ice cream to the base and freeze until completely frozen.

One hour before serving take the cake out so it has a chance to defrost a bit. Add fruits of your choice or chocolate chips or Maltesers, according to your preference. Remove the sides of the baking tin and serve.

Anicken Lundgaard

Poached Vanilla Pears

This easy yet impressive dessert can be served warm or chilled and perfect with a small scoop of vanilla ice cream.

 Serves 4    **Preparation time 30 mins**   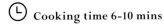 **Cooking time 6-10 mins**

Ingredients:

4 dessert pears

1 tsp runny honey (Australian or pure Scottish heather honey is great with this)

1 tsp vanilla extract

1 tbsp raspberries

Method

Peel each pear and cut in half. Scoop out the core but try to leave the stalk intact as this makes it easier to fish the pears our later.

Place in a heavy pan and barely cover with water. Add the honey and vanilla, simmering gently for 2 minutes, or until the pears are just tender. Stir in the raspberries, coating in the liquid. Lift out all the fruit (raspberries included) and place on a serving dish.

Boil down the remaining juices to form a syrup which coats the back of the stirring spoon, and pour over the fruit.

Serve warm or chilled.

Maggies Pudding Club

Cakes and Cookies

Chocolate Fudge Brownies

The addition of the fudge pieces and the hazelnuts makes these brownies just that little bit special.

 **Serves 6-8**   **Preparation time 15 mins**   **Cooking time 25-30 mins**

Ingredients:

250g unsalted butter

100g cocoa

500g golden caster sugar

4 eggs, beaten

100g self-raising flour

50 hazelnuts, chopped

100g fudge pieces

Method

Pre-heat the oven to 180C.

Line a baking tray with baking paper.

Put the butter, cocoa and sugar in a large saucepan and stir over a moderate heat until combined. Let the mixture cool slightly then add the beaten eggs a bit at a time and keep stirring.

Remove from the heat and add the flour, combining thoroughly. Add the chopped hazelnuts and fudge pieces.

Pour the mixture into the baking tray and bake for 30 minutes. Check and then cover with baking paper so the top doesn't burn and cook for another 15 minutes.

Leave to cool in the tin for 10 minutes, then turn onto a cooling rack.

Maggies Pudding Club

The Best Chocolate Brownies Ever

These brownies remind me of all the teenage parties we have been to in the last few years. I have been making them endlessly and keep on being asked to make more and more. They are the perfect pudding and especially for 'after party' munchies!! Delicious with ice cream and raspberries too.

 Serves 10    **Preparation time 15 mins**   **Cooking time 25-30 mins**

Ingredients:

300g butter

300 g of good quality dark chocolate, at least 70% cocoa solids

5 large eggs

450 g of granulated sugar

1 tbsp vanilla extract

200g plain flour

1 tsp salt

100g chopped nuts, milk chocolate buttons or cherries.

Method

Pre-heat the oven to 180C and line a 22-24cm square baking tin with baking paper.

Melt the butter and chocolate together in a heatproof bowl suspended over a saucepan of simmering water. Remove from the heat and cool slightly.

Beat the eggs, sugar and vanilla extract together in a bowl until the mixture is thick and creamy and coats the back of the spoon. Add the melted chocolate and butter and beat to combine.

Sift the flour and salt together and then add to the chocolate mixture, and continue to beat until smooth.

Stir in any nuts, milk chocolate buttons, or fruit (e.g. cherries) at this point.

Pour into the baking tin ensuring the mixture is evenly distributed in the tin and bake in the oven for 20 to 25 minutes.

To ensure moist and gooey brownies take them out of the oven, slide the knife into the mixture and it should come out coated.

Leave to cool before cutting into squares.

Emma Fletcher

Rocky Road

This is my favourite recipe. It's so easy to make and delicious to eat!

 Serves 10 **Preparation time 15 mins** **Chilling time 2 hrs**

Ingredients:

125g butter

150g milk chocolate

150g dark chocolate

3 tbsp golden syrup

200g rich tea biscuits

100 mini marshmallows

Method

Line an 18cm x 18cm baking tin with foil.

Place the biscuits in a re-sealable plastic bag and crush into smaller pieces but not too fine.

Melt the 2 types of chocolate, butter and golden syrup in a bowl over simmering water. (TIP: Warm the tablespoon under the hot tap so the golden syrup just slides off).

Fold the biscuit pieces and marshmallows into the chocolatey mixture and pour into the prepared tin. Put into the fridge to set.

Imy Lockhart - Age 14

Rocky Road

168

Malteser Tray Bake

My kids love this and even request it for their birthdays instead of traditional birthday cake. It's very easy to make and not only do the kids rave about it but it goes down well with adults too! A handy tip when you make this is to freeze the Maltesers beforehand as this stops their chocolate coating melting.

 Serves 8    **Preparation time 10 mins**   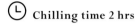 **Chilling time 2 hrs**

Ingredients:

100g butter

200g milk chocolate

3 tbsp golden syrup

225g finely crushed digestive biscuits

225g Maltesers

Method

You will need a swiss roll tin line lined with baking paper.

Crush the digestive biscuits in a food processor or in plastic bag using a rolling pin.

Melt together the butter, chocolate and syrup in a medium saucepan. Add the crushed biscuits and the Maltesers. Mix together quickly then pour into a lined swiss roll tin and chill until set.

For a special occasion drizzle with some melted white chocolate.

Fiona Yates

Chocolate Chip Cookies

These authentic American cookies are simple to make and extremely more-ish — so watch out!

 **Serves 15-20**   **Preparation time 20 mins**   **Cooking time 8-10 mins**

Ingredients:

1 block or 250g unsalted
   butter

1 cup caster sugar

1 packed cup light brown
   sugar

2 eggs, beaten

1 tsp vanilla extract

2½ cups plain flour

½ tsp salt

1 tsp bicarbonate of soda

1½ cups plain chocolate
   chunks

Method

Pre-heat the oven to 180C.

Lightly grease two shallow baking trays.

Place the butter, caster sugar and brown sugar in a large mixing bowl and cream until light and fluffy.

Beat the eggs and vanilla extract, and gradually beat into the butter and sugar mixture.

In a separate bowl, combine the flour, salt and bicarbonate of soda. Now add this to the butter mixture and mix thoroughly. Stir in the chocolate chunks.

Drop teaspoons of mixture onto the prepared baking sheets, ensuring there is sufficient room for the cookies to spread. Bake in the pre-heated oven for 8-10 minutes.

Remove from the baking sheet while still warm and cool on wire racks.

Elizabeth Green

Best Chocolate Cake in the World

This cake is a family favourite and my children always ask me to make it for their birthdays. I have also served it as a dessert with some fresh raspberries and ice cream. To save time I often decorate it with grated chocolate instead of making the chocolate curls.

 **Serves 8-10**    **Preparation time 20 mins**   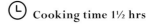 **Cooking time 1½ hrs**

Ingredients:

Cake

200g Bournville chocolate

125g butter

8 medium eggs, separated

200g golden caster sugar

Chocolate curls and ganache

200g Bournville chocolate

75mls double cream

25g butter

Method

Pre-heat the oven to 180C. Grease and line a 23cm spring-form tin.

Melt the chocolate and butter in a bowl over a pan of simmering water. Remove from heat and cool for a few minutes.

Put the egg yolks and sugar in the bowl of a freestanding mixer. Whisk together until pale and has a texture like mousse. Whisk in the chocolate and butter mixture.

Whisk the egg whites in a clean, grease-free bowl until soft peaks form. Add a third of this to the chocolate mixture and fold in using a large metal spoon. Add the remaining egg white and mix everything together, then pour into the prepared tin and bake in the oven for 1 hour 15 minutes.

Turn off the oven. Cover the cake with a damp tea towel and leave in the oven until the cake cools and the centre has sunk.

Meanwhile, to make the chocolate curls, melt half the chocolate in a bowl in a 900w microwave on high for about 1 minute. Pour into a small rectangular container and leave to cool so the chocolate hardens.

To make the ganache, put the remaining chocolate, cream and butter in a bowl and melt in a 900w microwave on high for 1-2 minutes. Mix together.

Take the cake out of the tin and peel off the paper. Put on a serving plate and ladle the ganache over so it covers the top of the cake and drizzles down the sides. Leave until just set.

To finish the chocolate curls, upturn the tub of cooled chocolate and pop the set chocolate block out of the container onto a board. Use a very sharp knife or vegetable peeler to scrape against the chocolate to make curls. Scatter over the cake.

Nicola Williams

Banana and Chocolate Chip Cake

This recipe was given to me by my sister and has become a great family favourite as well as being passed on to many other families. It is a good way of using up bananas and making an easy and delicious cake with little fuss. Great for tea time gatherings, lunch boxes and snacks.

 Serves 6-8  **Preparation time 15 mins** 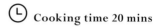 **Cooking time 20 mins**

Ingredients:

2 large ripe bananas, mashed

1½ tsp vanilla essence
   (optional)

175g margarine or butter

225g white sugar

275g self raising flour

1½ tsp bicarbonate of soda

3 eggs, beaten

125g chocolate chips

Method

Pre-heat the oven to 170C.

Grease a 20cm round, or 31cm x 23cm oblong cake tin.

Melt the margarine then add the sugar, beaten eggs, mashed banana, flour, bicarbonate of soda and lastly choc chips and mix thoroughly.

Transfer to the greased tin and bake in the oven for about 20 minutes until the top is springy to touch.

Liz Grant

Pear, Chocolate and Nut Cake

I found this recipe in an old magazine whilst desperately looking for new pear recipes as we had so many on our tree. It is quick and easy to make, delicious with cream, custard or ice-cream and can be eaten hot or cold so can be made a day or two in advance. It is popular with both adults and children so brilliant for a family lunch.

 Serves 8  **Preparation time 20 mins** 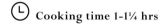 **Cooking time 1-1¼ hrs**

Ingredients:

Cake

125g hazelnuts

150g self-raising flour

175g butter

150g caster sugar

2 eggs, beaten

5 small pears, peeled

50g dark chocolate chunks

Glaze

2 tbsp apricot jam

Method

Pre-heat the oven to 180C.

Grease and line a 23cm round spring-form cake tin.

Grind the hazelnuts roughly to the size of breadcrumbs, this takes seconds in the food processor!

Add the flour and the sugar and combine thoroughly. Add the butter and beaten egg and continue to mix together.

Chop up 3 of the pears and stir into the mixture along with the chocolate chunks.

Pour the mixture into the prepared cake tin and decorate with the remaining pears, sliced into quarters.

Bake in the pre-heated oven for 1-1¼ hours until golden and firm to the touch.

Glaze with the melted apricot jam.

Serve hot or cold with double cream or crème fraîche.

Sarah Brown

Kirsty's Banana Bread

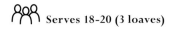 **Serves 18-20 (3 loaves)** 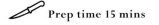 **Prep time 15 mins** 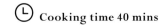 **Cooking time 40 mins**

Ingredients:

500g self-raising flour

200g caster sugar

250g butter

4 eggs

rind of one lemon

pinch of nutmeg

6 bananas

as many raisins and chopped
   walnuts as you like

Method

Pre-heat the oven to 180C.

Line 3 loaf tins with baking paper.

Put the bananas in a mixer and add all other ingredients except butter and blend. Melt the butter and pour in. Mix thoroughly.

Bake in the oven for about 40 minutes until golden brown on top and a skewer goes through the loaf cleanly.

Kirsty Wark – Journalist and Television Presenter

Blackcurrant Bakewell

This is a delicious, easy traybake which is simply sensational. Blackcurrant compote makes this even more tasty!

 Serves 18-20   **Preparation time 15 mins**   **Cooking time 40 mins**

Ingredients:

Sponge Base

250g butter

280g self-raising flour

250g golden caster sugar

½ tsp baking powder

4 eggs

150mls pot natural yogurt

1 tsp vanilla extract

Topping

1 tsp almond extract

4 tbsp blackcurrant jam

25g toasted flaked almonds

icing sugar to dust

Method

Pre-heat the oven to 180C.

Grease a 20x30cm baking tin and line with baking parchment.

To make the sponge, beat the butter, flour, sugar, baking powder, eggs, yogurt, vanilla and almond extract in a large bowl with an electric whisk until lump-free. Spoon into the tin and bake for 10 minutes.

Quickly dot over the jam, scatter over the almonds, then bake for 15-20 minutes more until golden and a skewer poked in the centre comes out clean. Cool in the tin, then dust with icing sugar.

Mel Leventis

Raspberry and Blackcurrant Cake

Lycopene and Ellagic acid are the stars of this easily-made cake. These pigments have been shown in clinical studies to limit damage caused by carcinogens. Although the levels of these potentially cancer-fighting chemicals found in this cake will not have a direct therapeutic benefit, including fruits (and vegetables!) in cakes will make them healthier overall. Most soft fruits would work in this cake, but the blackcurrants are particularly rich in antioxidants.

 **Serves 10-12**    **Preparation time 40 mins**   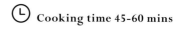 **Cooking time 45-60 mins**

Ingredients:

300g fresh or frozen raspberries and blackcurrants

First layer

150g unbleached plain flour

60g butter, melted

75g unrefined sugar, divided

1 tsp baking powder

¼ tsp salt

1 egg

1 tsp vanilla extract

Second layer

75g unrefined sugar

1 egg

1 tsp pure vanilla extract, divided

240mls plain low-fat or fat-free yogurt

4 tbsp unbleached plain flour

grated rind of one unwaxed lemon

Method

Pre-heat the oven to 170C.

Grease an 8 inch/23 cm loose-bottomed tin. Line the base with a circle of baking parchment. Set aside.

Thaw the fruit, if frozen, at room temperature for 30 minutes. Drain and pat dry the thawed berries.

In a medium mixing bowl combine the ingredients for the first layer of the cake. Mix well. This mixture is a paste so press evenly onto the bottom of the prepared tin.

Top the base with the berries.

In another bowl mix together the ingredients for the second layer and pour over the berries. A warning though: it will be runny.

Bake in the oven for 45 minute to 1 hour, or until the centre of the cake appears set and golden patches appear.

Cool in the tin on a wire cake rack for 30 minutes. Remove from the tin and cool completely.

Cover and refrigerate for 2 to 24 hours before serving. If serving this for a party, sieve over some icing sugar and surround with fresh berries.

Kellie Anderson - Nutrition Advisor Maggie's Cancer Caring Centres

Becky's Apple and Blackberry Square Cake

This delicious cake is a perfect tea time snack. For a variation, sprinkle 3 tablespoons of oat cereal over the mixture just before putting in the oven.

 Serves 6-8    **Preparation time 20 mins**   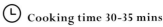 **Cooking time 30-35 mins**

Ingredients:

100g softened butter

175g self-raising flour

1 tsp baking powder

175g golden caster sugar

2 eggs

1 lemon, zest only

1 Cox's apple, peeled and diced

small handful of fresh blackberries

Method

Pre-heat the oven to 190C.

Grease a shallow 20cm square cake tin and line with baking parchment.

Place all the ingredients, except the apple and blackberries, into a large mixing bowl and beat with a wooden spoon until smooth. Carefully stir in the diced apple and blackberries. Spread the mixture evenly into the prepared tin.

Bake in the pre-heated oven for 30-35 min until golden and the centre is firm to the touch.

Leave in the tin for 10 minutes to cool before turning out onto a cooling rack.

Cut into small squares.

Maggies Pudding Club

Easy Fruit Muffins

This is a family favourite loved by all the children and grown ups. Not only are they authentic muffins, but they never fail! They are fruity, moist and very more-ish! They are best eaten on the day they are made and are hard to resist warm from the oven.

 Serves 12   **Preparation time 15 mins**   **Cooking time 25-30 mins**

Ingredients:

Muffins

2 cups plain flour

4 tsp baking powder

¼ tsp salt

½ cup caster sugar

100g butter

1 cup milk

1 egg

*1-1½ cups blueberries or
    chopped banana or thinly
    sliced apple etc.*

Topping

1 tbsp sugar

½ tsp cinnamon

Method

Pre-heat the oven to 180C.

You will need 12 muffin cases and a 12 hole muffin tin.

Sieve the flour, baking powder and salt into a large mixing bowl and add the caster sugar, mixing well.

Melt the butter gently in a medium saucepan. Add the milk and egg and beat to combine thoroughly. Add the fruit and liquid mixture to the mixing bowl containing the dry ingredients. Fold everything together, taking great care not to over mix. The flour should be dampened but the mixture should not be smooth. Scoop the mixture into each muffin case until about one half to three quarters full.

Make the topping by combining the sugar with the cinnamon. Sprinkle over the muffins.

Bake for 25-30 minutes until the muffins spring back when gently pressed in the centre.

Remove the muffins from the tin and allow to cool.

Kim Massam

Easy Fruit Muffins

Apple Dessert Cake

Always a favourite as a pudding or ideal for a coffee morning.

 Serves 6   **Preparation time 10 mins**   **Cooking time 1½ hrs**

Ingredients:

225g self-raising flour

1 level tsp baking powder

225g caster sugar

2 eggs

½ tsp almond extract

150g melted butter

350g cooking apples, peeled, cored and thickly sliced

25g flaked almonds

Method

Pre-heat the oven to 160C.

Lightly grease a deep 20cm loose-bottomed cake tin.

Mix the flour, baking powder, sugar, eggs, almond extract and melted butter in a bowl and beat for about a minute. Transfer half the mixture into the tin. Arrange the apple slices on top of the mixture in the tin, placing them mostly in the centre.

Spoon the remaining mixture over the apples. This may seem awkward but just make sure that the middle is covered well as the mixture spreads out in the oven. Sprinkle with flaked almonds.

Cook in the pre-heated oven for 1½ hours until golden and coming away from the sides of the tin.

Best served warm with ice-cream, or crème fraîche, dusted with icing sugar.

Amanda Gibbon

Oaty Apple Crumble Cake

This recipe brings back happy pre-children memories. My husband and I took our tandem to the Isle of Arran and enjoyed a tour, stopping off, as and when at a variety of "refuelling" cafes. This cake was served by one delightful woman, called Sally, and we dared to ask her for the recipe before heading off! Good with custard and nice cold!

 Serves 6    Preparation time 15 mins   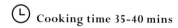 Cooking time 35-40 mins

Ingredients:

175g soft brown sugar

175g organic porridge oats

175g wholemeal self-raising
flour

1 tsp mixed spice

175g butter

225g cooking apples, thinly
sliced

Method

Pre-heat the oven to 180C.

Grease a 18cm loose-based cake tin.

Mix together the sugar, oats, flour and mixed spice in a bowl. Melt the butter and stir into the oat and flour mixture. Sprinkle half the mixture into the tin pressing down lightly. Arrange the apple on top and sprinkle with the remaining mixture, again pressing lightly.

Bake for 35-40 minutes.

Louise Hunt

Greek Orange Syrup Cake

This authentic Greek cake is a delight, having the consistency of a baked cheesecake. It is one of my staple recipes when I am entertaining as it is equally delicious served as a warm dessert with thick cream, or as a cake with afternoon tea.

Serves 8   **Preparation time 20 mins**   **Cooking time 35-40 mins**

Ingredients:

Cake

5 eggs

1 cup caster sugar

2 oranges, zest and juice

225g butter, melted

1 cup plain flour

3 tsp baking powder

Orange glaze

½ cup orange juice

½ cup granulated sugar

4 tbsp Grand Marnier liqueur
(optional)

Method

Pre-heat the oven to 180C.

Grease a 23cm spring form cake tin and line with baking parchment.

Firstly separate the eggs. Cream the egg yolks with the sugar and add the orange zest and juice. Stir in the melted butter then carefully fold in the sifted flour and baking powder.

Whisk the egg whites until they form soft peaks and then carefully fold into the cake mixture.

Pour the mixture into the prepared tin and bake in the oven for 35-40 minutes until golden and the cake is beginning to come away from the side of the cake tin.

Whilst cooking, make the orange glaze by combining the orange juice and sugar in a saucepan and simmer gently for 5 mins, stirring every now and again, until a light syrup forms. Remove from the heat and stir in the Grand Marnier.

Remove the cake from the oven and make a few holes in the top with a skewer. Now carefully spoon over the orange glaze

Annette McDonald

Olive Oil Cake

This is a beautifully light but flavorsome cake. It's such a doddle to make, it really shouldn't taste so good. Great served with cream and fresh berries.

 **Serves 8-10**    **Preparation time 15 mins**   **Cooking time 45 mins**

Ingredients:

Cake

4 eggs

200g caster sugar

grated zest of 2 lemons

250mls good olive oil

275g self-raising flour

Icing

juice of 2 lemons

100g icing sugar, sifted

Method

Pre-heat the oven to 190C. Grease and line a 23cm round, deep cake tin.

Put the eggs, sugar and lemon zest in a food processor and blend for 1 minute. Add the oil, through the funnel of the food processor, in a steady stream.

Place the flour in a mixing bowl and pour the egg and oil mixture onto to the flour, mixing all the while. Do not over mix.

Pour the cake batter into the cake tin and bake in the oven for 45 minutes, until a skewer inserted into the centre of the cake comes away cleanly.

To make the icing, add the lemon juice to the icing sugar and mix well.

When cooled slightly turn the cake out onto a wire rack and ice with the lemon icing.

Romilla Arber - Chef

Lemon Drizzle Cake

There is nothing like a warm lemon drizzle cake on a Sunday afternoon

 Serves 8    Preparation time 15 mins   Cooking time 40 mins

Ingredients:

Cake

225g unsalted butter, softened

225g caster sugar

4 medium eggs

finely grated zest of 1 lemon

225g self-raising flour

1 tbsp lemon curd

Drizzle topping

juice of ½ lemon

85g caster sugar

Method

Pre-heat the oven to 180C. Grease and line a loaf tin.

Beat together the butter and sugar until pale and creamy. Add the eggs one at a time, slowly mixing through. Add the lemon zest and lemon curd. Sift the flour and fold into the mixture. Spoon the mixture into the loaf tin and level the top with a spoon.

Bake in the oven for 35 – 45 minutes. Use a thin skewer inserted into the centre of the cake, if it comes out clean the cake is done.

While the cake is cooling in the tin, mix together the lemon juice and sugar to make the drizzle. Prick the warm cake all over with a skewer or fork, and pour over the drizzle. The juice will sink into the cake and the sugar will form a lovely crisp topping. Leave the cake in the tin until completely cool, then remove and serve.

The cake will keep in an airtight container for 3-4 days.

George Stow - Age 11

Lemon Squares

This recipe came from a cake making course I went on over 10 years ago and has been a favourite at coffee mornings ever since. It is quite hard to cut and can get a bit messy but when you taste it you will realise it is worth all the effort.

 **Serves 6-8**    **Preparation time 20 mins**   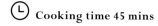 **Cooking time 45 mins**

Ingredients:

Shortbread base

225g plain flour

110g butter, softened

55g icing sugar

Lemon topping

225g sugar

2 eggs

2 tsp grated lemon peel

2 tbsp lemon juice

½ tsp baking powder

¼ tsp salt

Method

Pre-heat the oven to 180C and grease a square 20cm x 20cm x 5cm baking tin.

To make the base, mix the flour, butter and icing sugar in a food processor. Press into the baking tin and bake in the oven for 20 minutes until golden brown. Leave to cool.

Beat the topping ingredients together until light and fluffy, about 3 minutes. Pour over the cooled shortbread base (don't be tempted to add this when the base is warm as it will sink into the shortbread rather than sit on top). Bake in the oven for 25 minutes until set.

Cool in the tin and cut into squares.

Loida Almonte

Grandma's Fruit Loaf

A classic fruit loaf that is so easy to make. Great for those unexpected guests who turn up at the door! It brings back memories of many afternoons, sitting with a cuppa having a good old chat and a giggle with Grandma.

 **Serves 8-10**    **Preparation time 10 mins**    **Cooking time 1 hr**

Ingredients:

1 mug cold black tea (about 250mls)

225g dried fruit

225g self-raising flour

110g caster sugar

1 egg

2 tbsp marmalade

Method

Soak the fruit over night in the tea. The longer you can do this the better.

Pre-heat the oven to 180C.

Grease a loaf tin.

In a mixing bowl sieve the flour and add the sugar. Beat 1 egg and add that to the mixture along with the marmalade. Mix thoroughly and then add the fruit and the remaining tea that hasn't been soak up by the fruit.

Transfer to the loaf tin, bake for 1 hour or until a knife comes out clean.

Cool and cut into slices to serve.

Zoe Scott

Bran Fruit Loaf

I love this Bran Fruit Loaf and it always reminds me of my childhood as my Mum used to make this cake for the family. She still sometimes makes it for me now!

 Serves 6-8   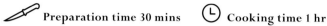 **Preparation time 30 mins**   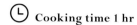 **Cooking time 1 hr**

Ingredients:

110g Kellogg's All Bran

150g caster sugar

275g mixed dried fruit

300mls milk

110g self-raising flour

Method

Pre-heat the oven to 180C.

Grease a 2lb (900g) loaf tin.

Put the All Bran, sugar and dried fruit into a basin, and mix them well together. Stir in milk and leave to stand for half-an-hour.

Sieve in the flour, mixing well and pour mixture into the loaf tin. Bake in the oven for about one hour. Turn out of tin and allow to cool.

Cut into slices and spread with butter.

Sarah Hindall

Norwegian Christmas Bread (Yule Kake)

Growing up in Norway we would eat this bread every Christmas Eve morning. Just a light breakfast in anticipation of the large Christmas meal we would devour later that day and the following days. The smell of the spices would fill the kitchen as we lightly toasted our slices and watched the butter melt into the bread.

 **Serves 6-8**    **Preparation time 40 mins**    **Cooking time 1 hr**

Ingredients:

500g caster sugar

250g butter

3 eggs

1 tsp ground cardamom (if you can't find ground in the shop, crush 8-10 pods, take out the "skin/pod" and crush the seeds by wrapping them in baking paper and rolling them with a rolling pin)

450mls single cream

250g raisins

100g Italian mixed peel (orange and lemon peel in syrup – baking section)

4 tsp vanilla sugar

900g flour

4 tsp baking powder

Method

Pre-heat the oven to 175C.

Beat the butter with the caster sugar in a food processor. Add the eggs one at the time.

Sift the flour with the baking powder and the cardamom and the vanilla sugar.

Take it in turns adding the flour and the cream to the mixture in the food processor. Empty the mixture into a large bowl and add the fruit. Split the dough in two and put in two buttered bread tins.

Bake in the oven for about one hour, until firm.

Eva Davies

Sponsored by

Classic Flapjacks

"I love these flapjacks in my lunch box because they are not too crunchy and not too soggy! They finish off my lunch nicely." Said Penelope Rushin age 9 ¾.

 Serves 6    **Preparation time 15 mins**   **Cooking time 20-25 mins**

Ingredients:

175g butter

150g golden syrup

50g light muscovado sugar

250g porridge oats (I use the cheaper small oats to prevent crumbling)

Method

Pre-heat oven to 180C.

Line the base of a 20cm square baking tin.

Melt the butter, syrup and sugar in a pan on a low heat, continually stirring the mixture. Remove from heat and stir in the oats. Press the mixture into the tin. Bake in the oven for 20 -25 minutes until golden. (Use longer cooking time for a crunchier flapjack).

Cool in tin for 5 minutes then mark into squares with a knife. Leave in the tin to cool completely before cutting and removing. (This prevents the flapjack from breaking up.)

Joanne Rushin

Gooey Goosh

Most people know this as "rice crispy squares" but in our family it has always been known "gooey goosh". It is a gooey, sticky mixture so beware, I once used a plastic spoon to mix it in the saucepan and when I pulled the spoon out half of it had melted with the toffees!

Serves 6   **Preparation time 20 mins**

Ingredients:

75g butter
110g creamy toffees
110g marshmallows
110g Rice Crispies

Method

Line a 20cm x 20cm square tin.

Melt the butter, toffees and marshmallows in a saucepan over a medium heat.

Add the Rice Crispies and mix well.

Turn the mixture into the tin (you need to do this quite quickly as it starts setting)

Leave to cool and cut into squares.

Hazel Hawkes

Rainbow Fairy Cakes

These colourful little cakes will brighten any tea time table!

 Serves 10    **Preparation time 15 mins**   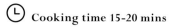 **Cooking time 15-20 mins**

Ingredients:

100g butter or margarine

100g caster sugar

2 eggs, beaten

100g self-raising flour

1 tsp vanilla essence

1 tsp of each food colouring:
red, yellow, green and blue

You will need 10 fairy cake cases or silicone moulds.

Method

Pre-heat the oven to 180C.

Cream the butter and sugar until pale and fluffy. Add the eggs a little at a time, beating well after each addition. Now add the vanilla essence. Gently fold in the flour using a metal spoon.

Divide the mixture into 5 bowls and add the food colouring to each, stirring well to give you red, orange (½ tsp red + ½ tsp yellow), yellow, green and blue.

Place a spoonful of the blue mixture in each fairy cake case or mould, followed with a spoonful each of the green, yellow, orange and red.

Bake in the oven for 15-20 minutes until springy to the touch.

Cool on a wire rack.

Wendy – Rainbow Trust

190

Bits and bobs

Barbecue Sauce

This is a very quick and easy sauce to make, so is ideal for those spur of the minute barbecues!

 Serves 8 **Preparation time 15 mins** **Cooking time 20 mins**

Ingredients:

1 onion, finely chopped

1 pepper, finely chopped

2 tbsp English mustard

2 tbsp brown sugar

tomato ketchup

Method

Heat a small amount of oil in a saucepan. Add the onion and fry gently over a low heat until soft. Stir in the mustard and brown sugar and cook for a couple of minutes. Add the chopped pepper and cook over a low heat. Add lots of ketchup, and cook very slowly over low heat for 20 minutes (do not let boil).

Serve with any barbecued meats.

Purée the sauce if you prefer it smooth.

Annabel Wilson

Pip's Barbecue Sauce

I learnt how to cook this barbecue sauce recipe when I was a chalet girl in Switzerland in 1991. I met a girl called Pippa who was a veteran chalet girl with three seasons behind her! When she discovered that I too was a backgammon player we became firm friends and she shared her famous " Pips barbecue sauce" recipe with me. All our 'punters' would ask us how we made it, but we just smugly smiled and never divulged the recipe!

 Serves 8-10   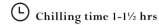 Preparation time 10 mins   Chilling time 1-1½ hrs

Ingredients:

8 tbsp water

110g sugar

110g tomato purée

2 onions, finely chopped

3 gloves garlic, crushed

4 tbsp olive oil

4 tbsp malt vinegar

6 tbsp redcurrant jelly

2 tins of tomatoes (800g)

salt and pepper

Method

Place the water and sugar in a heavy bottomed saucepan and boil until it begins to caramelise (big bubbles just starting to go brown around the edges.) Take off the heat and add the tomatoes. Stir until caramel has dissolved into the tomatoes. Add all other ingredients and simmer for 1-1½ hours.

Delicious hot or cold!!

Kate Hamilton-Bowker

Pip's Barbecue Sauce

Tomato Relish

 Serves 6  Preparation time 20 mins 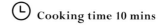 Cooking time 10 mins

Ingredients:

1kg ripe tomatoes

2 shallots, peeled and finely
  chopped

olive oil

sugar

malden salt

freshly ground black pepper

Method

Skin the tomatoes by cutting a little cross in their bottoms then drop them into rapidly boiling water for 30 seconds. Fish them out – their skins will now easily slip off.

Quarter the tomatoes, remove the seeds, then roughly chop the quarters into 1cm squares. Heat a little olive oil in a saucepan on the hob. Gently soften the shallot and garlic, now add the chopped tomato and over a low heat, simmer for 10 minutes.

Paul Clerehugh – Chef

Sunshine Dressing

The taste of this dressing makes me think of the South of France, a glowing sun, turquoise water and everything that can make life smooth and full of flavour.

 Serves 6-8 Preparation time 5 mins

Ingredients:

juice of ½ orange

olive oil

salt and pepper

Method

Squeeze the orange juice into a small measuring jug and add twice the amount of a not too strong olive oil and mix thoroughly. Add add salt and pepper.

Cecilia Kressner

Sunday Gravy

This is a real time saver, rather than the last minute panic of making gravy for your Sunday roast, this gravy can be cooked in advance and all you need to do is add the lovely meat juices when you take the roast out of the oven.

 Serves 10    **Preparation time 15 mins**   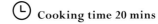 **Cooking time 20 mins**

Ingredients:

50g butter

1 large onion, chopped

2 medium carrots, chopped

5 beef Oxo cubes

1200mls hot water

150mls red wine (optional)

Method

Heat the butter in a large saucepan. Fry the onions and carrots on a medium heat until soft.

Dissolve the oxo cubes in 1.2 litres of boiling water. Add this to the onions and carrots. Add the wine if using and simmer for 30 minutes.

Blend in a liquidizer. Put aside.

Reheat the gravy when needed and add the juice from the meat roasting tin.

Freezes well.

Greta Davies

Avocado and Pomegranate Salsa

This is very good served with fish dishes where the fish is seared or griddled and is equally good with chicken cooked in a similar way or on a barbecue. The quantities can be adjusted to suit individual tastes and what I have set out is a guideline.

 Serves 5-6　　 **Preparation time 10 mins**

Ingredients:

3 ripe avocados

1 lime (increase to 2 if not
　very juicy)

1 pomegranate

generous handful of fresh
　coriander

fresh and coarsely ground
　black pepper

Method

Halve the avocados, remove the stones and peel away the skin. Chop into chunks about half an inch square.

Squeeze the lime and pour the juice over the chopped avocados. As some limes are juicier than others you may need to add the juice of a second lime.

Wash the coriander and chop coarsely. Combine with the avocado mixture.

Deseed the pomegranate discarding the tough outer skin and all the white pith dividing the segments of seeds. The pith is very bitter so make sure it is all removed.

Combine the pomegranate seeds with the avocado mixture and season with coarsely ground fresh black pepper.

Christine Sandall

Easy Cheesy Biscuits

Despite being literally stuffed full of calories these are deceptively light. I think these are better than chocolates to take as a gift, and make people optimistic about what is to follow, which has to be a good thing. They are easy to prepare ahead by keeping a sausage of the mixture in the fridge or freezer. If you aren't someone who prepares ahead, and I'm not, they take no time at all to make..

 **Serves 8-10**    **Preparation time 10 mins**   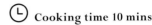 **Cooking time 10 mins**

Ingredients:

120g mature cheddar cheese

120g unsalted butter

120g strong plain flour, sifted

pinch cayenne pepper

1 egg

Method

Pre-heat the oven to 230C.

Place the cheese, butter, flour and cayenne pepper in a food processor and blitz until it just comes together. Lightly knead into a cylinder shape (the size of a £2 coin).

Cut into thin slices approximately 2mm thick.

Place on a lightly greased baking tray, leaving space between them to expand.

Brush with the beaten egg and bake for 10 mins.

Rosie Reid

Sarah's Fabulous Fudge

Fudge has always been one of my favourite sweet treats and every Saturday morning I used to go down to the newsagents and spend my 50p pocket money on a packet of fudge. Then one day, once Mum trusted me enough to cook in the kitchen, I attempted to make it myself. The result was excellent and now, whenever I come home from boarding school my brothers always ask me to make some. I hope you enjoy this recipe as much as I do

 **Serves 6-8**    **Preparation time 20 mins**   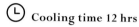 **Cooling time 12 hrs**

Ingredients:

550g golden caster sugar

500mls double cream

3 tbsp liquid glucose

140g white chocolate, cut
　　into chunks (not too small
　　or they'll melt completely)

Method

Line a 22 cm square non-stick tin with baking parchment.

Put the caster sugar, double cream and liquid glucose in a pan. Slowly heat together, stirring continually, until the sugar melts and stops felling grainy on the bottom of the pan. Turn up the heat and fast boil until a small amount of the mixture dropped into a glass of cold water sets into a soft ball that you can pick up on a teaspoon. By this time the bubbles in the mixture will look small and even.

Turn off the heat and keep stirring for 5 minutes or until the mix starts to thicken a little.

Sprinkle in the white chocolate and swirl it through the mixture once using a spatula or the handle of a wooden spoon. Pour into a tin and leave the fudge overnight to set, then turn out and cut into squares.

Will keep for up to 2 months in an airtight container, don't store in the fridge or the fudge will go soft.

Sarah Woodard – Age 15

Best Breakfast Ever

So easy, so healthy and so delicious

 Serves 2    **Preparation time 10 mins**   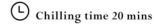 **Chilling time 20 mins**

Ingredients:

1 handful of rolled oats

1 grated apple or pear

1 or 2 squeezes of lemon juice

8-10 tbsp of natural yoghurt

honey to taste

fruits and berries to taste, but here are some ideas:

raisins – best if put in with the rest the evening before eating

cranberries – best if put in with the rest the evening before eating

blueberries or other berries – put in just before eating

kiwi – chop up just before eating

bananas – chop up just before eating

Method

Grate the apple or pear roughly, add the lemon and orange juice, then the yoghurt and the honey. Add raisins or cranberries if you like these. Put in the fridge overnight.

Add any other fruits you like in the morning just before eating.

The best thing about this recipe is that you adapt it to what you like and what fruit you have in the fruit bowl! You do need the lemon and orange juice to stop the apple going brown. And I use Yeo Valley Organic Yoghurt as it is so creamy and delicious.

Philippa Wiggin

Richards' Mulled Wine

For many years my parents had "open house" on the Sunday before Christmas when mulled wine would be served. I was intoxicated by the smell long before I was allowed to drink alcohol. Latterly I helped with the preparation and have headed my father's words ever since —"Less is more". This could not be simpler and is the better for that.

 Serves 6    Preparation time 15 mins

Ingredients:

1 bottle of ordinary red wine
   (Merlot, Shiraz, Cabernet,
   blend – whatever grape
   you like)

1 small stick of cinnamon

6 cloves

50-100g granulated sugar

½ glass brandy

ground nutmeg (optional)

Method

NO oranges, they make it go cloudy!

Pour the wine into a large saucepan; add the cloves and stick of cinnamon. Very slowly bring the wine to near boiling and add the sugar to taste.

Allow to simmer, bearing in mind that the longer the wine mulls the more flavour will infuse from the cloves and the cinnamon, and the more alcohol will be lost in the steam!

Decant the hot mixture into a large jug.

Just before serving add half a glass of cooking brandy to the jug (add it earlier and the aroma and alcohol of the brandy will be lost).

Stephen Richards

Simon's Bullshot

This recipe is now legendary on the Yattendon shoot. You are guaranteed to be very popular when you bring out a flask of this on a cold winter morning! Beware though as it does contain quite a bit of alcohol.

 **Serves 8-10**   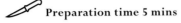 **Preparation time 5 mins**

Ingredients:

2 cans consommé soup

600mls chicken stock

1 glass sherry

3 shot glasses of vodka

good splash of Tabasco

1 tbsp Thai fish sauce

seasoning (salt, paprika,
  cayenne pepper, black
  pepper etc)

Method

Put all the ingredients except the vodka in a pan and heat until boiling. Add the vodka, reheat and pour into a warmed thermos flask.

Simon Gordon

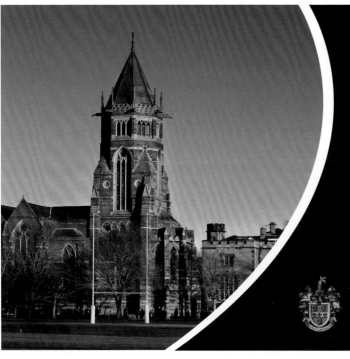

Mugs, jugs and more.

Perfect pottery for family cooking.

From the renowned Ceramika Artystyczna Pottery in Boleslawiec, Poland. Suitable as both table and ovenware, the thick stoneware is high-fired using non-toxic, ecologically-safe paints and glazes, resulting in a smooth, durable finish that is oven, Aga, microwave and dishwasher-safe.

This beautiful hand-decorated pottery is a stunning yet practical addition to any table.

www.mugsjugs.moonfruit.com

Or contact Emma Armstrong:

mugsjugs@hotmail.co.uk

Tel: 01189 724406

Also see the website for forthcoming Fairs

Emma Armstrong, Ashdown House, Chiltern Road, Peppard Common, Henley-on-Thames RG9 5HX

THE
ROYAL
OAK

THE ROYAL OAK
YATTENDON

A beautiful, authentic country pub with rooms offering:

Stunning, Michelin rated, home cooked food
Delicious Sunday roasts
Fixed price lunch menu Monday to Friday
Award winning real ales
7 luxurious guest bedrooms

Glorious walled beer garden
Al fresco dining under leafy vine terrace
3 roaring log fires
4 private dining rooms for up to 70 guests
Boules piste

Accreditations include:
The Michelin Guide 2011
The AA Good Pub Guide 2011
Alistair Sawday's Special Places To Stay 2011
The Good Beer Guide (CAMRA) 2012
Britain's Finest Hotels 2011

The Royal Oak | The Square | Yattendon | Berkshire | RG18 0UF
Telephone 01635 201325 | Email info@royaloak.com | Website www.royaloakyattendon.co.uk
GUBB INNS LTD, THE ROYAL OAK, THE SQUARE, YATTENDON, BERKSHIRE, RG18 0UF
REGISTERED IN ENGLAND & WALES NO 7079019